Stephe Chambers

Hay-on-Wye

August 1989

GLASGOW UNIVERSITY PUBLICATIONS

XXVIII

THE POPULATION OF ATHENS IN THE FIFTH AND FOURTH CENTURIES B.C.

A. W. GOMME

Lecturer in Greek in the University of Glasgow

ARGONAUT, INC., PUBLISHERS

CHICAGO   MCMLXVII

Library of Congress Catalogue Card No. 67-31062

Unchanged reprint of the original edition Oxford 1933

CONTENTS

I. TOTAL FIGURES AND CLASS DISTRIBUTION

II. COUNTRY AND TOWN POPULATION

NOTE A

The Value of Athenian Statistics. The Bouleutai Lists

NOTE B

The Epheboi and Diaitetai Inscriptions

NOTE C

The Size of Athenian Families, and the Exposure of Children

Contents

THE POPULATION OF ATHENS

I

TOTAL FIGURES AND CLASS DISTRIBUTION

THERE is no subject of the first importance in ancient scholarship in which our thoughts are vaguer, in which we almost refuse to think (because the evidence is unsatisfactory), than that of population. That it is of great importance we cannot deny : not only because it would be of value to know the resources in man-power of the Greek states in comparison with each other, with Persia, with Rome, or with modern states ; but chiefly because it would, obviously, add so much to the vividness and truth of our picture of Greece, and of Athens in particular, if we could give even approximate answers to three questions : (1) how was the population distributed ? that is, into rich and poor, into citizen and foreigner, into free and slave, and into town-dwellers and country-dwellers. (2) How did it fluctuate ? for example, how much was it affected by war and emigration in cleruchies between 480 and 430 ? What was the net loss due to the Peloponnesian War ? Did the population increase again during the fourth century, between 400 and 322, and how quickly did it decline after that ? And (3), perhaps the most interesting question, because of the peculiarities of the Athenian constitution : if the assertion of the oligarchs in 411 that no more than 5000 citizens ever attended the ecclesia was not wildly untrue, what proportion was that of the whole number ? And what proportion of the whole were the dicasts ? Again, in the Boule of 500 a member served for a year, and could only be reëlected once—could not therefore serve for more than two years in all. Therefore, even assuming that everyone who was elected once served also a second time (and we know this was not so), 250 new men were required every year. They had to be over 30 ; suppose 40 was the average age at election—how many citizens in Athens reached the age of 40 every year, what proportion of this number was 250 ? At least 250 again would finally retire from membership of the Boule every year : on the same assumptions, that every member served twice and 40 was the average age of election, and supposing 65 to be the average age at death,[1] there were at all times over 6000 men who had had two years' experience of political affairs as members of the highest council of the state—the executive committee, as it were, of Athens, who did all the day-to-day business of the city, who received foreign ambassadors, who worked with the strategoi, the treasurers, and other officials, and prepared the business for the ecclesia. What proportion was 6000 of the whole ?—or of that active part of the citizen-body who attended the ecclesia and the law-courts ? Clearly these crowded, jostling, mass-meetings, which decided important political or judicial questions, did not consist only of the ignorant and the inexperienced —the cuckoos who were easily gulled by a Pericles or a Cleophon.

All of these are highly interesting and important questions, which cry out for answers. It is true that no certain or exact answer can be given to anyone of them, owing to the paucity and weakness of the evidence. We have few direct statements on the matter, and many even of these are exasperatingly disputable. But we cannot simply ignore the whole problem : we must make what we can of the evidence at our disposal. The object of this paper is an analysis of that evidence. Such an analysis, systematically done, has already been attempted by Beloch, to whom all honour is due ; and no fresh evidence has come to light since he last wrote. But I differ from him often in method and sometimes in result ; and a new analysis is wanted.[2]

[1] In Western European countries the expectation of life of a man of 40 has increased from 26 to 30 years within the last half-century.
[2] Cavaignac's work, though it contains many interesting calculations, is so wanting in system that his results are mostly guesswork.

We have six *kinds* or groups of evidence :

(A) Vague, general statements, such as the 30,000 citizens in 500 B.C. given by Herodotus ; but the figure soon became so completely conventional that it is not worth discussion, even though it may have been based originally on a fairly accurate estimate.[1]

(B) Precise statements, by many authorities, competent and incompetent, of army strengths. Thucydides and, to a less degree, Xenophon, and Polybius for a later age, are among the former ; Herodotus, and expecially Plutarch and Diodorus (whose value varies according to the authorities he is following) among the latter. But, in the first place, manuscript figures are peculiarly liable to corruption ; and secondly, we can seldom be certain whether the figure given represents effective strength (those actually taking part in a campaign— given in round numbers), or estimated strength, the strength, that is, of the classes called up, including therefore many who, through temporary absence or illness, through exemption in consequence of other duty, or by malingering, escaped service. (I do not propose to discuss the supposition of Beloch and others that the figures represent paper-strength in the full sense of the word—that is, every one of the relevant ages living. This paper strength was known, and easily ascertainable by a historian, from the κατάλογοι of hoplites, and from the ληξιαρχικὰ γραμματεῖα kept by the demes.[2] But since every hoplite served in the ranks as a fighting unit, among the front-line troops, was, as we should say, on the " bayonet-strength " of the army, none in any auxiliary force, and moreover marched and fought in

---

[1] How conventional it became is seen from the 30,000 audience in the theatre of Dionysus that held not more than 13,000, an audience that included women and children and foreigners (Plato, *Symp.* 175 E), and the 30,000 average *population* of states in Menander, *Epit.* 653 ff., that is all men, women and children, citizen and foreign, slave and free. Similarly with the 20,000 of Ps.-Dem. xxv 50 : cf. the 20,000 citizens of prehistoric Athens in Plato, *Critias* 112 D.

[2] The metics also were registered in their demes and so could be counted.

heavy armour, it is clear that between the ages of 20
and 50 there must have been many men unfit for active
service. In modern countries, in war-time, men between
40 and 50 are not, normally, placed among the front-line
troops, but in the auxiliary services (when called up at
all) ; and in antiquity—in Rome for example—men over
40 were not normally called up for foreign service ; it
was only because the population of Athens was too small
for the fulfilment of her imperial ambitions, that so
exacting a call was made on her citizens. Whether the
names of men permanently unfit were kept on the
κατάλογος or not, we do not know ; but in any case there
must have been a large discrepancy between the paper-
strength of the hoplite army (as defined above—the
total of men between 20 and 50) and the estimated or
the effective strength when a mobilization in full force
(πανδημεί, πανστρατιᾷ) took place. If Beloch's con-
tention were true, none of the figures given us, even by
Thucydides, would be worth much more than the conventional figures of Herodotus. But though there is
indeed a certain conventionality about all ancient figures
of armies, quite apart from the use of round numbers
only : for example Thucydides often ignores all casualties
of a campaign except those actually recorded for a
battlefield ; yet this only means that we are not dealing
with exact figures : in everything, even the least uncertain element, a margin of error of at least 5% either
way is understood ; and that being so, we may go on
our way.)

1. Our most precise figures for the hoplite force, both
active and reserve, are those given by Thucydides (ii 13,
6–9) for 431 B.C. These have indeed been disputed, and
emended by many scholars, including Beloch ; but I have
defended the MS. tradition at length elsewhere,[1] and

---

[1] *C.Q.* xxi (1927) 142—151. It has been conjectured as well (e.g.
by Cavaignac) that the 16,000 reserve included some 8–10,000 cleruchs,
settled in different parts of the empire. But this view, besides being open
to most of the criticism brought against Beloch's emendation, is directly
contradictory to Thucydides' words ; who says that the 16,000 were
available for defence of the walls of Athens and Piraeus.

need here only observe that Beloch's emendation, to read 6,000 for 16,000 in the reserve, involves two assumptions, (1) that when Thucydides says 13,000 hoplites invaded the Megarid in 431, he meant 8 or 9,000, and (2) that he either includes unfit men in the effective strength or ignores them altogether, even in the reserve ; or else that there were no men in Athens of 50 and under (even after the plague) who were not fit for active service in the infantry. This remarkable result I refuse to believe ; the more readily as it is only attained by the alteration of a particularly well-attested reading.

Thucydides' figures then, tell us that in 431 Athens had 14-15,000 active troops of hoplite census or over (13,000 infantry, 1000 cavalry, and the troops in frontier forts whose number is not given), and 16,000 in the reserve, including the metic hoplites ; and that 13,000 citizen infantry were in fact in the field later in the same year. The total of metics is not given (our first difficulty); but since 3000 of them took part in a small sector of the active operations, with the citizen army, and they were, in all probability, not so thoroughly organized as the citizens (this was their first campaign abroad, many of them will have been but recently settled in Athens, and they were, technically, all in the reserve), we may assume that there were at least 2000 or 2500 more— unorganised, unfit and old—of hoplite census : say 5,500 in all.[1] This leaves us with about 14,500 citizens in the active army and 10,500 (16,000 less 5,500) in the reserve —25,000 citizens of hoplite and cavalry rank between the ages of 20 and 60.[2] The active army consists of fit men between 20 and 50, the reserve of men of 18—19 and 50—60, and of the unfit (all other men on the register).[3]

---

[1] It is generally assumed that the 3000 who took part in the Megara campaign are the total number of metics of hoplite census between 20 and 50 (or even between 20 and 60). This is both unnecessary and improbable.

[2] For the summary of all the figures, see the table below, p. 26.

[3] Thucydides calls all the reserve " the oldest and youngest," a loose expression. That he did not really suppose that the numbers of men of 18 19 and 50 60 were equal or nearly equal to those between

For the period before the Peloponnesian War we have
only Herodotus' statement (ix 28) that there were 8000
Athenian hoplites at Plataea (when the thetes, and
doubtless also many of hoplite rank, were serving in the
fleet), and that of Thucydides (i 107. 5) that the hoplites
in the Athenian army at Tanagra numbered 14,000, of
whom 1000 were Argives, and an indefinite number
" other allies."

2. In the plague of the years 430–29 and 426–5 Athens
lost more than one-quarter of her first-line troops (300
cavalry and 4,400 hoplites " from the regiments "—
Thuc. iii 87) ; there were other losses in battle (which
would not all be made up by new recruits, for the losses
in the plague among boys of 14—18 will have been
equally severe) and by emigration, but not more than
1500 in all.   This would leave less than 11,500 first line
troops, citizen and metic, out of the 17,500 (14,500 and
3000 metics of 431) ; in fact, when Athens put forth
her full strength in 424 she could muster not more than
9,500—10,000 men.[1] The plague had left many men
enfeebled and disabled, and the proportion of the unfit
among the men of military age must have been exceptionally large.   On the basis of the figures of 431 B.C.,
11,500 first-line troops would imply a total of c. 20,000
men between 18 and 60, of whom c. 4,000 will be metics :
a figures however which should be increased somewhat,
for though the plague must have been more often fatal
to the old than to the young (as to Pericles, and not to
Thucydides), yet the older men were not reduced in
number by fighting and emigration.   So some 16,500

20 and 50 (as some have foolishly thought) is shown by v 64. 3, where
he estimates the oldest and youngest of the Spartan army in the field
to be one-sixth of the whole.   We may perhaps compare also v 72. 4,
τῶν Ἀργείων τοῖς πρεσβυτέροις καὶ πέντε λόχοις ὠνομασμένοις (contrasted
with οἱ χίλιοι λογάδες just above).   And certainly the " oldest and
youngest " Athenians who defeated the Corinthians in 458 (Thuc. i
105. 4) were not exclusively men of 18—19 and 50—60.

  [1] C.Q. 1927, p. 149 f. (there were troops elsewhere, besides those
at Delion).   Thucydides, in Thrace at the time of the battle, had only
Boeotian sources for his figures for Delion (iv 90, 94) : the Athenian
hoplites were equal to the enemy, their irregular levies, light-armed
and unarmed, were considerably larger.

citizens of 18—60, of hoplite and cavalry census, in 425, and, say, 4000 metics.[1]

The story in Lysias (xx 13) about the well-meaning oligarch Polystratus perhaps implies that there were only 9,000 citizens of this rank in 411. That is only an orator's statement, and that orator Lysias ; but it is not impossibly inconsistent with the above figure. There had been further heavy and recent losses in war, the number of men reaching the age of 20 every year was still greatly affected by the losses of the plague ; and numbers of men of hoplite census may have been much reduced by the impoverishment brought about, especially in the agricultural population, by the long years of warfare. It is, however, a very probable suggestion of Ferguson's, that these 9000 are men over 30.[2]

3. The years 411—403 saw more impoverishment and heavy losses in battle and in the revolution (for which our figures are not well attested) ; and the decline in the birth-rate due to the losses between 431 and 423 was further affecting the number of new recruits. Athens made a remarkable and rapid recovery in material prosperity in the fourth century. She was able to put 6000 hoplites and 600 cavalry in the field in 394 (Xenophon, *Hell.* iv 2. 17), and again in 368 and 362 in support of Sparta (Diodorus, xv 68. 2, 84. 2). But now the figures are less useful : Diodorus is not a good authority (he gives 12,000 for the campaign of 369—xv 63.2—where Xenophon says only that the Athenians sent their full force) ; we do not know the proportion of metics (quite possibly there were none ; they did not often serve with the regular army abroad) ; nor how many first-line troops were kept in Attica at a time when Boeotia, though

---

[1] Diodorus (xii 58. 1), that is, Ephorus, had slightly different figures for the losses from the plague, as he had for the army-strength of 431 (cf. *C.Q.* 1927, pp. 143–4) ; but they appear to be conventional : over 4000 τῶν στρατιωτῶν, 400 cavalry, and of the rest, slave and free, more than 10,000. There must have been far more than 10,000 if slaves are included, even if males only are considered. Thucydides says the numbers dead of the rest were not counted.

[2] In *Camb. Anc. Hist.* V. 338.

not openly at war, was hostile and at war with the allies of Athens. But for 323-2 we are more fortunate : Diodorus (xviii 10. 2, 11. 3—now following a good source) says that 5000 foot and 500 horse were sent out in the campaign against Antipater of Macedon ; these were men of 21—40 only, not 21—50, and from only seven of the ten Athenian regiments, the other three being kept at home to guard Attica. This means about 7000 foot and 700 cavalry for the whole army up to 40 ; and there would not be many men between 41—50 fit for active service, not more than a thousand ; a total of first line troops therefore of about 8,500, giving, on the basis of the figures for 431 B.C., some 14,500 hoplites of 18—60. Or, by a different route, 7,700 men in the field implies at least 9,000 men living between 20 and 40 (allowing for the unfit and the exempt—trierarchs, office-holders and others). On modern analogy of age-distribution,[1] this should mean 14,000—15,000 men between 18 and 60, of hoplite and cavalry census.[2]

(C) *The evidence of inscriptions.* About 335 B.C. was carried the reform providing for a more thorough organisation and training for the recruits of 18 and 19 years old, now perhaps for the first time officially styled *epheboi.*[3] We have a few, very few, official figures

---

[1] See below, pp. 75 ff.

[2] Diodorus implies that the whole force at Lamia consisted of citizen troops ; this may well be true ; but we cannot be certain that it did not include metics.

[3] See A. Brenot, *Recherches sur l'éphébie attique.* I cannot agree that the institution was first established in this year, as Mlle Brenot, following Wilamowitz and others, believes. The language of Aeschines, ii 167 (ἐκ μὲν γὰρ παίδων ἀπαλλαγεὶς περίπολος τῆς χώρας ταύτης ἐγενόμην δύ᾽ ἔτη, καὶ τούτων ὑμῖν τοὺς συνεφήβους καὶ τοὺς ἄρχοντας ἡμῶν μάρτυρας παρέξομαι· πρώτην δ᾽ ἐξελθὼν στρατείαν, κ.τ.λ.) is decisive, together with Aristotle's use of περιπολεῖν τὴν χώραν (*Const. Ath.* 42. 4) as one of the duties of the epheboi, and references to the oath taken by them in the temple of Aglaurus in Lycurgus, c. *Leocr.* 76 (ὑμῖν γὰρ ἔστιν ὅρκος, ὃν ὀμνύουσι πάντες οἱ πολῖται, ἐπειδὰν εἰς τὸ ληξιαρχικὸν γραμματεῖον ἐγγραφῶσι καὶ ἔφηβοι γένωνται), Dem. xix 303, and Plut. *Alcib.* 15. 4. Mlle. Brenot argues that συνέφηβοι in Aeschines does not mean "fellow-epheboi," but only men of the same age, and that Aeschines was in some mercenary corps (of which we hear nothing from other sources of this period). But it matters nothing that συνέφηβοι is perhaps not a technical term. All we need to know is that Aeschines and other Athenians of the age 18 and 19 served

giving the number of the epheboi from each deme. (It is part of the irony of things that we have far more evidence of this kind for later centuries, from the third century down to Imperial times, when not only was Athens of less importance, but the evidence is of no value for an enquiry into population, for only a small proportion of those available was then recruited.) One such list gives us about 45 names from Kekropis in 334 B.C., that is those who were entered as epheboi on reaching the age of 18 in that year ; another gives us 63 names from Leontis in 327 or 326 ; a third about 33 names from Erechtheis in 305 (when there were 12 phylae).[1] If the phylae had each an equal number of hoplites, or if these phylae had an average number, we should have to assume 450 epheboi in all in 334, 630 in 327–6, c. 400 in 305. We can believe that a reorganized institution worked better in 327 than in 334 ; it is almost certain that in the confused years after 322 there was a fall in population (particularly of the young and active who would go off to Asia), and in all probability a decline in efficiency and in enthusiasm.[2] It is possible as well

on garrison duty of some kind, under Athenian officers. Thucydides' use of οἱ νεώτεροι for a particular class of soldiers not normally sent on service abroad points to a similar arrangement in the fifth century. (Mlle. Brenot, pp. 5—7, has some remarkable ideas about the Athenian army organisation, before 335—the soldiers got no training at all ; that is why the Athenians early gave up the practice of carrying arms on all occasions). That Thucydides could use περίπολος in a different sense (iv 67. 2, viii 92, 2), and that a περιπόλαρχος at the end of the fourth century was probably in command of mercenary troops (*I.G.* ii[2] 1193), proves nothing against taking Aeschines' words in their natural sense. (In 352/1 B.C. the peripolarchos, with the strategos ἐπὶ τὴν φυλακὴν and other officials, had the duty of guarding sacred lands—*I.G.* ii[2], 204[20] ; he may have commanded the citizen recruits.) That there was a reorganisation in or about 335 is not denied ; the precise duties of the epheboi in each of their two years of service and the relationship of the strategoi to them, were then probably better defined, and, to judge from Plato, *Rep.* 537A—B, *Legg.* 755C, 760C, 772A, the offices of kosmetes and sophronistes to the epheboi established.

[1] For a discussion of these inscriptions, especially the second, and a few other doubtful fragments, see below, Note B. It should however be stated here that most scholars believe the Leontis epheboi to be those of both years (18 and 19), which would considerably affect the figures.

[2] The population, in the census of Demetrius of Phaleron, was less by a third than the probable population of 322 (below, p. 18). This suits the epheboi-figure for 305 well enough, except that we would

that Leontis was somewhat larger than Kekropis,[1] or had a larger proportion of citizens of hoplite census. It would be unsafe to assume a yearly average of less than 500 recruits, or rather boys reaching their 18th year, for the period 334—323 ; the figure should probably be a little higher. On modern analogy, 500 of the age of 18 would give c. 13,000 hoplites between 18 and 60, to which have to be added a small number, 1000 or so, for the cavalry, who were trained separately. This gives a figure sufficiently near the estimate based on Diodorus' figures for the Lamian War to encourage us. Since 500 appears to be the minimum number, I would prefer to put the figure of all those of hoplite and cavalry census of 18—60 at c. 15,000.[2]

On the other hand, a complete list of *diaitetai*, men who served as arbitrators in their 60th year, for 325-4 B.C. (the only complete and only certain list we have[3]) gives us 103 names. If this were all or nearly all the men of 60 in that year, it would mean not more than 7,000 men between 18—60 ; this is obviously too low, and we must suppose a number of exemptions from service as arbitrators, as likely as not because not more than a certain number was required ; and therefore ignore this evidence in our calculations.

It is clear that we have nothing like enough evidence for the epheboi to give us *confidence* ; we have not enough that is to justify an average, especially as we

suppose a greater proportionate decline in the thetes than in the hoplite class.

[1] Cf. below, p. 50.

[2] In Greece in 1918–22, with a population of a little over 5,000,000, there was a yearly recruitment of c. 35,000 (*Times*, April 18, 1927 ; letter on the population of Turkey). On this basis a recruitment of 500 would mean a population of 72–75,000 and a total of males of 18—60 of c. 19,000. Doubtless the *hoplite* population of ancient Athens was healthier and more thoroughly recruited than the total population of modern Greece. The *Statesman's Yearbook* for 1931 gives 60,000, with a population of over 6,000,000—doubtless a paper figure of those reaching the age of 18.

(Tarn, in *Camb. Anc. Hist.* vi. 442, and vii. 78—this latter for the year 300 B.C.—, gives 800 as the annual recruitment. I do not know on what evidence he bases this figure.)

[3] See below, Note B, p. 70.

are dealing with low figures where normal variation has a disproportionate effect on the mean. But the figures we have are consistent enough with those of Diodorus ; and it is possible that the margin of error, one way or the other, is not very wide. There is of course no pretension to exactness : a possible error of 500 or even 1000 either way in a suggested total of 15,000 is understood.

It must however be emphasized that this comparatively satisfactory result is attained by assuming that only men of the hoplite census were enrolled as epheboi (and diaitetai). This is almost certainly right[1] ; but Aristotle, our chief authority for the details of the ephebeia, and writing just at this time, implies that all citizens were enrolled (*Const. of Ath.* c. 42)[2] ; just as he implies that all citizens on reaching their 60th year were liable to service as arbitrators (c. 53). This would not greatly affect the credibility of Diodorus' figures, for the army of 323 would include 12—14 classes of men recruited since the reform ; but the ephebic and arbitrators' lists would give an impossibly small total for the whole citizen population ; and in addition Athens still had a considerable fleet, some 200 vessels, in which the citizens of the poorest class (as well as metics and foreigners) served—the fleet which was finally defeated at Amorgos in 322. The thetes then did not actually form part of the army of Lamia, and had probably not been trained as hoplites ; and we must assume that Aristotle forgot to state that they were excluded from the ranks of the epheboi (and of the arbitrators) because such a fact was well-known and obvious to his readers[3] : an assumption in itself unsatisfactory.

If however it is correct, we have fairly consistent (and therefore, as they are drawn from many sources, credible) figures for the hoplite population of Athens ; from which we conclude a rapid growth between 480 and 431

[1] So Busolt, Beloch, Sundwall and others.
[2] So does Lycurgus, *c. Leocr.* 76 (see above, p. 8, n. 3).
[3] Deloch, *Gr. Gesch,* 402.

(whether due in the main to natural increase or to increase of prosperity by which large numbers of thetes joined the hoplite ranks, we do not know), very severe losses (in the plague, in fighting and from impoverishment) between 431 and 403, and a slower increase from that date to 323–2, perhaps chiefly due to a greater prosperity.[1] We may perhaps connect with this reckoning the fact that marriage between Athenians and foreigners was legal until 451 (how common, we do not know) and the children of such marriages full citizens ; after 451 it was not recognized and the children were metics, the change, being due, according to Aristotle, to the rapid growth of the population (*Const. Ath.* 26. 4) ; the law was relaxed during the Peloponnesian War, but re-enacted in all its rigour in 403–2 and remained thereafter in force : only children both of whose parents were Athenian became citizens.

(D) These approximate figures, however, are of citizens of the hoplite census only ; we have no similar figures for the poorest class of citizens, the thetes. We know that their military duty was to serve as rowers (and probably also as epibatai) in the fleet ; we know the numbers of ships at sea on various occasions, especially during the Peloponnesian war, and the size of the crews. But metics and foreigners also served as rowers ; and we do not know in what proportion.[2] A large number

[1] Beloch (*Gesch.*, 402 f.) accounts for the increase in the field army between 362 and 323 by supposing that after the reform of 337–5 all epheboi from the Athenian colonies at Lemnos, Imbros, Scyros and Samos came to Athens for their training, as Epicurus did, and that the cleruch hoplites were called up for the Lamian campaign, and not for Mantineia. This is only guessing. Epicurus at 18 may have wanted to come to Athens.

[2] In the fourth century at least there was a κατάλογος of men liable to service as rowers (Dem. 50. 5, 16). How the thetes were enrolled in the fifth century is unknown : Thuc. vi. 26. 2 suggests κατάλογοι of seamen as well as of hoplites ; but one would suppose from other expressions of Thucydides that no muster-roll was kept—ὁ ἄλλος ὅμιλος ψιλῶν οὐκ ὀλίγος of the Megarid campaign (ii 31. 2) ; ψιλοὶ δὲ ἐκ παρασκευῆς μὲν ὡπλισμένοι οὔτε τότε (424 B.C.) παρῆσαν οὔτε ἐγένοντο τῇ πόλει· οἵπερ δὲ ξυνεσέβαλον ὄντες πολλαπλάσιοι τῶν ἐναντίων (iv 94. 1) ; and of the losses by the plague, after precise figures for the cavalry and hoplite regiments, τοῦ δὲ ἄλλου ὁμίλου ἀνεξεύρετος ἀριθμός (iii 87). Yet the num-

of the rowers were non-citizens in prosperous times certainly, as between 431 and 413 ; there was a larger proportion of citizens between 413 and 405, and probably in the fourth century than in the fifth (cf. Dem. xlvii and l). But we cannot get even approximate figures. All we can say is that in the fifth century a considerable number of rowers were citizens (Arist. *Ach.* 162, *Equit.* 551 ff.; Thuc. vi 31 ; cf. Ar. *Pol.* iv. 4. 1, 1291 b[1]), many were metics (Ps.-Xen. *Resp. Ath.* i. 12 ; Thuc. vii 63. 3), a very few slaves (Ps.-Xen. i. 19 ; cf. Thuc. viii 73. 5 and i 55)—mostly the servants, probably, of the ship's officers,—and a large number, probably the majority, foreigners (generally from the subject allies in the days of the empire) attracted by Athenian rates of pay, till higher pay was offered by the enemy.[2]

1. In the autumn of 428, when Athens was suffering severely from the plague, the Peloponnesians planned a sudden attack by sea on the Piraeus. Seventy Athenian vessels were elsewhere, doubtless also some others, ten at least, on routine duties ; but by enrolling citizen and metic hoplites, the Athenians were able to put to sea with 100 ships and make a demonstration sufficiently imposing to discourage the enemy. It was only a demonstration ; but even so, sufficiently remarkable, for the hoplites could not have been trained oarsmen.[3]

bers of voters was ascertainable from the deme-lists ; and the fleet was well-organised then, and the names of those who served known ; of those who fell recorded equally with the hoplites. It is because citizens, metics and foreigners all served together as light-armed and in the fleet, that Thucydides gives no figures.

[1] The passage from the *Politics* should be quoted for the sake of those who still believe that the masses in Greek states lived as minor state officials : εἴδη γὰρ πλείω τοῦ τε δήμου καὶ τῶν λεγομένων γνωρίμων ἐστίν, οἶον δήμου μὲν οἱ γεωργοί, ἕτερον δὲ τὸ περὶ τὰς τέχνας, ἄλλο δὲ τὸ ἀγοραῖον τὸ περὶ ὠνὴν καὶ πρᾶσιν διατρῖβον, ἄλλο δὲ τὸ περὶ τὴν θάλατταν, καὶ τούτου τὸ μὲν πολεμικὸν τὸ δὲ χρηματιστικὸν τὸ δὲ πορθμευτικὸν τὸ δ' ἁλιευτικὸν (πολλαχοῦ γὰρ ἕκαστα τούτων πολύοχλα, οἶον ἁλιεῖς μὲν ἐν Τάραντι καὶ Βυζαντίῳ, τριηρικὸν δὲ 'Αθήνησιν, ἐμπορικὸν δὲ ἐν Αἰγίνῃ καὶ Χίῳ, πορθμικὸν ἐν Τενέδῳ), πρὸς δὲ τούτοις τὸ χερνητικὸν καὶ τὸ μικρὰν ἔχον οὐσίαν ὥστε μὴ δύνασθαι σχολάζειν.

[2] Thuc. i 121, 143. 1—2 ; Xen. *Hell.* i 5. 4 ff., 20. See Ed. Meyer, *Wehrkraft* 168 ff.

[3] Thuc. iii 16 ; cf. 3. 2, 7. 1, 13. 3. Note that even at this crisis slaves were not called upon, proving not only that normally they did not serve, but also that unskilled men were enrolled as sparingly as possible.

The 80 ships already at sea required 800 epibatai and some 13,500 rowers. Suppose not more than 30 per cent. of the latter to have been citizens and metics, and the citizens to have been only a little more numerous than the metics, and we have c. 3,300 citizens (800 + 2,500) on service. The 100 ships required 1000 epibatai (who on this occasion would all be hoplites) and 17,000 rowers ; such a number could not be found amongst the regular and trained men available at the Piraeus—hence the enrolment of hoplites.[1]   Not more, certainly, than one-quarter of the crews could have been hoplites, or the untrained men would have destroyed the mobility of the ships : let us suppose 13,000 out of the 17,000 to have been trained men, citizens, metics and foreigners. Even so we do not know the proportion of each class. If the foreign sailors, present in the Piraeus for such emergencies, did not amount to more than 50 per cent. of the 13,000, we have 6,500 to be divided between the remaining metics of thetic class, and citizens, say 5,000 citizens and 1500 metics. That is, at this time, there would be 8–9000 thetes on active service ; therefore *at least* 13,000 men between 18 and 60 of the thetic census (men quite unfit to row would be numerous, and there must have been large numbers left engaged in various industries) in 428, and so 16–17,000 in 431, to which are to be added the 1800 archers (Thuc. ii 13. 8), and the unfit and old ex-archers—at least 18,000 in all in 431.[2]   It is obvious however that such figures are the result of very rough estimates, and have little value, though I think the figure 18,000 may stand as a minimum. I have discussed them to show the uncertain nature of our ground, and because they have been used as evidence for some surprising figures by so good an historian as Meyer.[3]

[1] Unless the hoplites were only to serve as ephibatai, this duty normally being done by thetes.

[2] Table, p. 26, col. 2.

[3] *Wehrkraft*, p. 170–2 : he assumes, unnecessarily, that all the 17,000 rowers (and 800 officers) in the 100 ships were citizens and metics, of whom 6000 would be zeugitae ; that of the 12,000 in the 70 ships half were citizens and metics (perhaps too large a proportion) ; that is c. 18,000 in all. Further, that there were more metics in 431 than in

2. In 351 the ecclesia voted a decree to send a fleet of 40 vessels against Philip in Thrace and to call up the classes to 45 for the manning of them (Dem. iii 4). Demosthenes' words (καὶ τοὺς μέχρι πέντε καὶ τετταράκοντ᾽ ἐτῶν αὐτοὺς ἐμβαίνειν) should mean that only citizens were to be called up, and imply that to man 40 triremes it would be necessary to enrol practically the whole number of trained rowers and marines (for few men over 45 would be fit for active service) ; that is that the number of trained and fit men was about 8,000. Even so, we do not know in what proportion these stood to the total number of thetes, whether or not in a proportion similar to that of the first-line hoplites and the total of the hoplite-census. Law court speeches of this period suggest the service for the fleet was badly organised and the standard of efficiency low (e.g. Dem. c. *Polyclem*). And the value of this piece of evidence is sensibly diminished by the fact that the resolution of the ecclesia was never carried out ; so that we remain ignorant of what its effect would have been.[1]

3. Nor are our figures for light-armed troops used on land any better. Thucydides refuses to give the number of those who joined in the Megara campaign of 431 ; Herodotus says there were 8000 at Plataea (at a time when large numbers of Athenians were serving on the fleet), but only on the rough and ready principle of one light-armed soldier to every hoplite ; at Delion in 424 there were " considerably more " than 10,000 (see above,

313 B.C., when there were 10,000 (see below), that there were more poor metics in proportion to rich among the metics than among the citizens (a quite gratuitous assumption : the reverse is equally possible—men came to Athens in search of wealth, and would leave if they did not find it) ; that therefore, as there were 3000 metic hoplites in 431 (see above, p. 5), there were " at least " 9000 metic rowers. Therefore about 6000 in 428 ; therefore 12,000 citizen thetes rowing in 428, and 18,000 in 431. He supposes a total of thetes over 18 of 25,000, leaving only 7000 who are not fit and trained rowers, which is not enough. Later (p. 179), for other reasons, he has to reduce this total to 20,000.

[1] Beloch, who makes use of this passage (*Gr. Gesch.* 398) has to suppose that metics are included in αὐτούς and to suggest that the age-limit 45 is a MS. error (or a mistake by Demosthenes) for 35, in order to make this evidence fit in with that of other writers. It would be wiser to ignore the passage.

p. 6, n. 1). Not only are the numbers vague, but we do not at all know the proportion of citizens ; at Delion for example, a muster was made of every available man— citizen, metic and foreigner. But the majority of the " light-armed " (unarmed, most of them) were hastily collected for a few days' urgent fortification work, and returned home before the battle. When not only metics, but foreigners staying at the moment in Athens, were called up, it is idle to pretend that we can extract from a total anyhow vague the number of citizen thetes. We are driven back on a fifth class of evidence, definite but not always trustworthy statements about the total adult male population.

(E) 1. A gift of 3c,000 medimni of corn was made to Athens in 445–4 by a Libyan prince, for distribution among the citizens. Philochorus (fr. 90) is reported by a scholiast on Aristophanes (*Vesp.* 718) to have said that 14,240 citizens each received a gift,[1] and that it was discovered that 4,760 persons had falsely represented themselves as citizens and claimed their share ; and they were prosecuted. Plutarch (*Per.* 37) says that the gift was of 40,000 medimni, that the numerous lawsuits resulted in " nearly 5,000 " men being condemned for wrongly claiming citizenship and sold as slaves, and that the total number of citizens remaining was 14,040 (probably a MS. error only, for 14,240). Two things are clear : (1) that of Philochorus' two figures (which together make exactly 19,000) one is only inferred by deducting the other from this round number ; and perhaps the figure of those who received a share is the one documented, for it is less probable that the exact number of men struck off the citizen roll, or the exact number of lawsuits, was recorded : the number of those to receive corn would be known for purposes of distribution, or

---

[1] To add to our difficulties, the Scholiast tells us that each man is said to have received five medimni, which, as he says, does not agree with the other figures. I suspect the figure 30,000, which looks like an estimate based on one medimnos for each of the traditional 30,000 citizens ; Plutarch's figure is different.

was calculated by dividing the 30,000 medimni by the quota received by each citizen.[1] (2) That 14,240, as a figure for the total of citizens in 445–4, is irreconcilable with all our other evidence, and with the facts of the Peloponnesian War; incidentally the constitution would have been unworkable. But it is a possible figure for the total of those who got a share of the dole, if only the poorest applied, and those only who lived in or near Athens; and perhaps not individual citizens, but heads of families; and probably not Philochorus, but Plutarch only identified them with the whole body of citizens—" als ob Kleon und Sophokles und die ratsheern und Areopagiten mit einem scheffelsack in das Odeion zu den getreidemessern gelaufen wären."[2] But, equally, we must not take 14,240 as an exact figure for the thetic class, for we may be sure that many a zeugite would have been glad of a gift of two or three medimni of corn (7—8 medimni being a year's consumption for one man).

3. In 322 B.C., after the crushing defeats at Amorgos and Crannon, the Athenian constitution was changed at the bidding of Antipater : henceforth only those citizens with property worth 2000 dr. (the old limit of the zeugitae) were to retain full rights. We are given figures, by Plutarch (*Phoc.* 28) and by Diodorus (xviii 18. 5, from a good source) ; but there is a discrepancy. 9000 citi-

---

[1] Beloch, *Bevölkerung* 75 ff. But no probable quota divided into 30,000 (or 40,000) would produce 14,240 ; and the story implies that this last figure was only ascertained some time after the distribution of the corn. Nor, incidentally, does 30,000 or 40,000 divide easily into 19,000.

[2] Wilamowitz, *A. u. A.* ii 209. Gernet, *l'Approvisionnement,* 276 ff., arguing that such distributions were made regularly to all citizens (Dem. xxxiv 39 ; *I.G.* ii² 647), tries to accept the figure by referring it to a corn-distribution of 424 B.C. (see same Schol. ad *Vesp.* 718). But a distribution in that year is doubtful, and 14,000 still an impossible figure : there were more hoplite citizens than that (see above). See R. L. Sargent, *Number of Slaves*, p. 61, n. 89, who quotes Plaut. *Aulul.* 107—112 to show that probably thetes only shared in such a gift of corn.

Equally unsatisfactory for our purpose is the story of Diphilus' property, 160 talents : how it was confiscated when Diphilus was impeached by Lycurgus (the date is unknown—between 345 and 325 B.C.) and distributed among the citizens at the rate of 50 dr., or, " as others say," 100 dr. each (Ps.-Plut. *Vit. X Orr.* 843 D). These figures give 19,200 and 9,600 citizens respectively.

B

zens remained ; 12,000 were disfranchised according to
Plutarch, 22,000 according to Diodorus.[1]   It is clear
that it is the latter figure only which is consistent with
the statistics of Lamian War discussed above ; the
former may be a MS. error ; more probably it is an in-
ference from the figures of Demetrius' census (see below).
The proportion of citizens worth more than 2000 dr. is
surprisingly low ; but this was an oligarchic reaction and
the property so valued may have been land only, the
only wealth considered by men of Aristotle's school to
constitute a claim to citizenship.[2] Whether the figures
refer to men over 18, or to voters, over 20, we do not
know. 31,000 men over 18 would mean 28–29,000 of
18–60.   If the figure 14–15,000 for those of hoplite
census of 18–60 in 323–2 (above, p. 10) is approximately
correct, we have remaining about an equal number of
thetes.

4. During the rule of Demetrius of Phaleron (317–307)
a census was taken τῶν κατοικούντων τὴν Ἀττικήν,
which, according to Ctesicles as quoted by Athenaeus
(vi 272 c.), gave 21,000 citizens, 10,000 metics and 400,000
slaves. The last figure is certainly wrong,[3] but the others
are not affected by this. The exact date and the object
of the census are not known, but it has been plausibly
conjectured, since only adult males were counted (at

---

[1] The text of Diodorus has been emended to make it agree with
Plutarch, and is in consequence often misquoted, as by Cary, *J. H. S.*
1928, p. 225 ; who points out that about this time citizen rights at
Cyrene too were confined to men possessed of 2000 dr. or more.

[2] 2000 dr. represents an income of 200 dr. a year, or a net yield
of 200 medimni of corn in the old days, with corn at 1 dr. the medimnus.
But wheat was now about 6 dr., barley 3 dr. (barley being the chief
cereal grown in Attica) ; and there were olives and vines. We cannot
believe that only 9000 citizens were worth 200 dr. a year in 322.

[3] Athenaeus quotes from Aristotle the figure 470,000 for the slaves
in Aegina " at one time," and from Timaeus 460,000 for those in Corinth.
The former figure is fantastic ; the island could never, at the most
favourable moment of her trade, have supported a total population of
more than 70–80,000 ; and according to Aristotle himself (see p. 13, n. 1,
above) large numbers of poor citizens engaged in commerce, leaving
but little room for slaves. (It is not the MS. of Athenaeus which is
corrupt—cf. 272 E ; but Athenaeus probably misread the earlier figures :
though, it must be confessed, they support one another.)

least of the citizens and metics), that, like those at Megalopolis and Rhodes about the same time, it was desired
to obtain the number of men of military age in case of
a siege (such as threatened Athens in 313).[1]   If so, the
figures will give the number of men, or of fit men,[2]
between 18 and 60.   21,000 citizens between those ages
would imply about 24,000 over 18 and 22,500 over 20 ;
perhaps more, if only men capable of taking an active
part in the defence of the city are included ; in any case
a considerable decline in population from the 31,000 of
322 B.C.   This is what we should expect.   The wide
dispersion of Greeks after Alexander's conquests in Asia
will have affected Athens as other Greek cities, especially
after the failure in the Lamian War ; and we are told
that many of the citizens disfranchised in 322 were given
lands and settled by Antipater in Thrace (Diod. xviii
18. 4 ; Plut. *Phoc.* 28).

Metics and foreigners.   In the article already quoted
I argued that there may have been 5,500 metics between
18 and 60 of the hoplite census in 431 B.C. (see above,
p. 5).   How many poor metics there were we have no
means of knowing ; we can only say that they must
have been numerous.   They were engaged in many
manual trades, and they formed a considerable proportion of the crews of Athenian fleets (cf. Nicias' address
to them in Sicily, Thuc. vii 63. 3).[3]   The 10,000 metics
of 313 B.C. presumably include foreigners temporarily
resident, at least all who could be pressed into service[4] ;
but they may not have been many of them.   We cannot
argue from one age to another ; for the number of metics
would tend to vary more than the citizens : in times of
difficulty many men, not yet rooted in Attica, would

---

[1] Beloch, *Gesch.* 405.

[2] Fit for any kind of war service, in the ranks, in the reserve
(garrison duty) or in auxiliary services, according to the Megalopolis
census (Diod. xviii 70. 1). For the Rhodian census, see Diod. xx 84. 2—3.

[3] Cf. also Ps.-Xen. *Ath. Rep.* cited above, p. 13.

[4] They are expressly mentioned in the account of the Rhodian
census (Diod. xx 84. 2).

leave for more tempting fields ; as Isocrates complains that the city was " deserted by its merchants and foreigners and metics " during the Social War of 357–5 (viii 21). We may therefore assume that there were far fewer metics in 400 than in 431 ; that their numbers increased, though very irregularly, during the prosperous times of the fourth century ; that there were consideraby more than 10,000 in 330 ; and that after 313 the number probably still further declined. But we cannot say more than that.

For the average number of foreigners temporarily resident in Athens at various epochs we have no evidence ; we can only say, from the frequent mention of them, that it was not negligible. I have inserted the empty column in the table on p. 26, as a reminder that they are to be taken into account.[1]

Slaves. We have only three figures from antiquity to help us estimate the slave population : the first suggests only a very rough estimate ; and of the other two one is probably, the other certainly false.

1. In the Decelean War Athens was much injured by the desertion of more than 20,000 slaves, the majority of whom were engaged in industry ($\chi\epsilon\iota\rho\sigma\tau\acute{\epsilon}\chi\nu\alpha\iota$; that is, were not casual labourers, nor domestic servants : Thuc. vii 27. 3–5). If by " the majority " is meant, say, 13–14,000, we may suppose that there were not more than 40–50,000 engaged in industry altogether (Xenophon says there were in the fifth century more than

---

[1] The large part played by the foreign element in Athens, both metic and non-resident, is shown by the number of their tombstones. In the fifth century, of some 150 names so recorded, at least 40 are of foreigners ; in the following centuries (IV—I) over 700 are certainly foreign, compared with some 1050 certainly citizen. (These last figures from Clerc, p. 379, based on the first edition of *I. G.*) The very large majority of the tombstones have been found in Athens and Peiraeus where the metics were concentrated ; and we must not draw any con-clusions as to the proportion of metics to citizens.

It is interesting to note that on these tombstones of metics, which were the private affair of the family, we have no mention of the demes to which they belonged : that showed only their position in the Athenian state.

10,000 in the mines[1]), or the loss would not have been felt so acutely. In 431, as we have seen, there were probably some 27,000 citizens (over 20) and perhaps 6000 metics of the hoplite and cavalry classes. Every hoplite and cavalryman seems to have taken a servant with him on campaign[2]; but we cannot suppose a much higher average than one male domestic servant to each adult (which is a good deal more than one to each family); we may therefore conclude that 85,000 (50,000 plus 35,000) is the upper limit for the number of male slaves in the most prosperous times of the fifth century. There may have been another 35–40,000 female slaves in domestic service.[3] This is putting the total at its highest : it means that on the average a family with two grown-up sons (assuming that the grown-up daughters were successfully married off) had four servants. We may be sure that many hoplite families could not afford so many. The number of domestic slaves among the thetes must have been negligible : servants are expensive to keep. It will be seen that these figures are largely guess-work, as indeed must be the " more than 20,000 " of Thucydides : who made that estimate ?

2. In the crisis after Chaeroneia Hypereides proposed (and carried in the ecclesia) a decree to enfranchise and arm all disfranchised citizens, all metics and the slaves ; and Suidas in his lexicon quoting (at second or third hand) a sentence from the speech he made when later

---

[1] *Vectig.* 4. 24–5. Xenophon is a poor authority, but there was apparently a slave-tax imposed on owners of slaves used in the mines (*ibid.*), so their number could have been known.

Suppose there were 30,000 slaves in industry in addition to the miners : 25 hands in a factory meant it was a large one, and the owner well-to-do ; 30,000 would mean 1200 factories with 25 hands each as an average. I do not believe that there were in fact so many.

[2] Thuc. iii 17. 4. See Sargent, *Class. Phil.* xxii 1927, 201–12, 264–79, for the use of slaves in war-time.

[3] Hardly any, as far as we know, in factories ; but since much spinning and weaving was done at home, and by slaves in the richer households, there may have been more women than men slaves in domestic service. And there were doubtless others, wives of slaves carrying on small businesses of their own, retail shopkeepers and the like (cf. the manumission inscriptions ; below, p. 42).

impeached for his proposal gives the number of slaves as 150,000 (no figures being given for the disfranchised and the metics) ; that is 150,000 adult male slaves.[1]   All that we know or can reasonably infer of Athens at this time argues against the correctness of this figure ; it is much too high.   It has been suggested to emend to 50,000,[2] taking this to be the number (and a very rough estimate at that) of those who could usefully be armed : which would imply perhaps some 70,000 male slaves in all—which is indeed an acceptable enough figure.   But the method of reaching it is unsatisfactory.   There would be fewer women slaves than in 431, for even if luxury had increased (which is doubtful), the free population had declined.   (Cols. 10, 11, 12 of the table, p. 26 ; such evidence as we have shows an increase of slaves in industry compared with free men : cf. below, p. 40, n. 2).

3. The figure 400,000 for the male slave population in 313 (above p. 18) would mean an average of about thirteen slaves (in addition to slave women) to every free man, citizen and metic, rich and poor, in a time of declining prosperity and population, in a city where, in prosperous times, a factory employing 20 hands was accounted a large one, and the owner of 45 slaves engaged in industry was a very rich man ; and an enormous and not credible increase on the figures for the much more prosperous period a quarter of a century before, even if we accept 150,000 from Hypereides.   It is in fact quite inconsistent with the latter figure.

The numbers of the slave population must have oscillated more frequently and more violently than that of the free.   Slaves were, almost all of them, bought from abroad, not born and reared in Attica, and were employed (when not in domestic service) in factories and mines, where employment was most liable to fluctuations, not in a basic industry such as agriculture.

[1] Hypereides, fr. 29.
[2] Beloch, *Gesch.* p. 415–6.   I am not enamoured of the suggestion.

The man who invested capital in the purchase of slaves was in a different position from the hirer of free labour and the modern owner of machinery : for in times of bad trade they were not only idle, but had to be fed and housed at least well enough to keep them fit ; they became a burden ; whereas the hirer of labourers was no longer responsible for his men when once the contract was over. If a man owned slaves trained to a particular craft, their profitable employment depended not only on a general prosperity, but on the prosperity of that industry : so that unskilled slaves who could be turned on to any work were a less speculative investment than skilled, though the latter were more profitable when continuously employed. We know very little of the conditions of the regular slave market ; but slaves were cheap to buy, and not, apparently, dearer in the fourth than in the fifth century, as were corn and other staple articles. The price too might vary suddenly, if a large number of slaves was thrown on the market as the result of a military campaign. Two or three minae was a common price ; yet it was reckoned that the slaves in successful factories would bring in each a net profit of 60–80 dr. at least per annum ; we hear even of 120 dr. ; and unskilled labourers in the mines brought in 60 dr.[1] : that is a return on capital of 20–50 per cent., at a time when money earned not more than 8–10 per cent. ; and the interest-bearing life of a slave could be reckoned on the average as 25 years (against which must be set an idle period at the end of his life if he had not purchased his freedom). The reason for this high return was partly, in very prosperous times in Athens, as between 480 and 430, simply the abundance both of the supply and of the opportunities for profitable employment ; but also, in more uncertain times, this very danger of finding yourself with idle slaves on your hands. Not only were men reluctant to invest a large sum on the purchase of a slave, however skilful, whose constant employment was un-

[1] Dem. xxvii 9, 18 ; Aeschin. i 97 ; Xen. *Vectig*. 4. 14. See Beloch, *Gesch*. iii 1, p. 319.

certain ; but in a crisis many owners would hurry to sell to save the cost of upkeep, a fact which would tend to keep prices down. Many a man must have been relieved when his slaves ran away to the Spartans at Decelea. This must be the chief reason why slaves cost no more in the fourth than in the fifth century : the recovery of Athens from the disasters of the Peloponnesian War was remarkable, but the growth of prosperity was not steady as it seems to have been in the fifth century, but fluctuated from one decade to another.

We must not therefore argue from one age to another, except in a most general way—we can be certain for instance that there were far more slaves in Athens in 430 than in 480, and more in 338 than in 313 ; that therefore, if there were 400,000 in 313 (even supposing this to include women—see above, p. 18 f.), there were far more than 150,000 in 338. We should not be at all surprised if there were twice as many in 338 as in 313—so greatly might the slave population fluctuate. But we are quite without evidence as to the extent of these fluctuations and we must be on our guard in making assumptions.[1]

We have some further evidence, which, though tantalizingly inadequate, yet affords us some measure of control—figures of corn production in Attica and of imports of foreign corn, which can give us a rough idea of the total consumption and hence of the total population. We will first tabulate the results—uncertain as they are—which we have so far obtained ; I will say, by way of preface, that I regard the figures for citizens as *minima* in every case, those for slaves as *maxima*.

[1] Gernet, for example, p. 289 ff., one of the few modern writers who keep the figure 400,000, argues that the number is not too many for a free population (men, women and children) of 150–180,000 — his figure for 430 B.C. But the 400,000 slaves belongs to the census of Demetrius ; and we must take the figure to be true of that year or not at all. Of course an average of 13 for every citizen and metic (more than 13 per family) is ridiculous. Has Gernet ever thought of the cost of housing, feeding, and clothing them ? He speaks of the public slaves, who " employés dans les fonctions multiples de l'administration, étaient particulièrement nombreux " : how many thousands ? What was the budget figure for their keep ?

NOTES TO TABLE I

(1) Based roughly on the 8000 at Plataea and a calculation of the possible increase of citizen population between 480 and 430, checked as this was by wars and emigration. Possibly this increase given above is too large, and the figures for 480 too small.

(2) A very rough guess, based on the number of ships at Salamis and Mycale (which must have been manned mostly by citizens). The total citizen population in 500 must have been large to make Cleisthenes' constitution workable (Wilamowitz, *Arist. u. Athen.* ii 207–8), and perhaps nearer to that of 430 than is suggested in this table. The thetes may well have decreased in number between 480—430 owing to wars and emigration in colonies and cleruchies, and to an increase of prosperity and consequent rise of many to the hoplite class. (The fall in the value of money would also increase the number nominally belonging to the hoplite class—those worth 200 dr. a year; but it would not increase the number capable of providing their own arms.)

(3) Col. 4. For this column (based on a multiplication of the number of men 18—59 by 4), see Note C, below, pp. 75 ff.

(4) Col. 8. For the total of metics in 431 I have multiplied the number of men of 18—59 by 3, insteaf of by 4 as in the case of the citizens, for there must have been large numbers of men newly settled without the normal proportion of women and children. For 338 and 313, when they had been much longer established, I have multiplied by 3½. In 313 the proportion would have been nearer to 1 in 4, for many metics must have sought their fortunes in the East before their families moved there. See below, p. 82.

(5) It is useless to guess at the numbers of metics and slaves at the beginning of the fifth century. They were much smaller than in 431 ; there may have been very few metics indeed, only some hundreds, for the majority of foreigners who had settled in Athens in the course of the sixth century had been enfranchised ; and the story of the hurried rebuilding of the walls of Athens in 479 does not suggest a large supply of slave-labour.

(6) I have included this column, although we cannot make a guess at the number of these foreigners at any date, in order to draw attention to them. They must have been numerous—several thousands—in the time of the empire, between 450 and 413, as rowers in the fleet and as traders. In the fourth century there would have been fewer rowers, but probably more traders. In 400 their number must have been negligible ; and in 313 probably quite small.

(7) It is generally assumed that there were more poor metics than rich, and more proportionately than poor citizens. This is quite uncertain, especially for the fifth century, when probably more men came to Athens as traders than as labourers. But we cannot be sure, and this total for metics may be by a good deal too small. See below. (We have another piece of tantalizingly dubious evidence. In an εἰσφορά the metics paid τὸ ἕκτον μέρος—Dem. xxii. 61. It is commonly believed—as by Clerc, p. 24—32, and recently by Hommel in Pauly-Wissowa, s. v. *Metoikoi*—that this means that the metics as a body paid one-sixth of the total sum raised by the tax, the citizens paying the other five-sixths ; and that since the metics numbered very many more than one-sixth of the total free population, and were taxed at least as heavily as the citizens, they must have been on the whole much poorer and there must have been many more poor metics than well-to-do. But the meaning of this ἕκτον μέρος is very doubtful. The language of Demosthenes does

TABLE I

| Date | CITIZENS | | | | METICS | | | | | SLAVES | | | | Total Population of Attica. |
| | Men 18–59. | | | Total of Citizens. (3) | Men 18–59. | | | Total of Metics. (4) | Foreigners temporarily resident. (6) | Men. | | Women. | Total of Slaves. | |
	Hoplite Census and Over.	Thetes.	Total.		Hoplite Census and Over.	Thetic.	Total.			Domestic.	Industrial.	Domestic.		
480	15,000 ? (1)	20,000 ? (2)	35,000 ?	140,000	?	?	?	? (5)	—	?	?	?	? (5)	?
431	25,000	18,000 ?	43,000 ?	172,000	5,500	4,000 ? (7)	9,500 ?	28,500	?	30,000 ?	50,000 ?	35,000 ?	115,000	315,500
425	16,500	12,500 ?	29,000 ?	116,000	4,000 (8)	3,000 ? (8)	7,000 ?	21,000	?	22,000 ? (8)	37,000 ? (8)	22,000 ? (8)	81,000	218,000
400	11,000 ? (9)	11,000 ?	22,000 ?	90,000 ?	?	?	?	? (10)	—	?	?	? (10)	? (10)	?
323	14,500	13,500	28,000	112,000	?	?	12,000 ? (11)	42,000	?	20,000 ?	60,000 ?	24,000 ?	104,000	258,000
313	12,000 ? (12)	9,000 ? (12)	21,000	84,000	?	?	10,000	35,000	—	?	?	?	?	?
	1	2	3	4	5	6	7	8	9	10	11	12	13	14

not at all support the above interpretation : Androtion abused some citizen—πάντων ἀκουόντων ὑμῶν ἐν τῷ δήμῳ δοῦλον ἔφη καὶ ἐκ δούλων εἶναι καὶ προσήκειν αὐτῷ τὸ ἕκτον μέρος εἰσφέρειν μετὰ τῶν μετοίκων.)

(8) Based only on the assumption that the losses of the metics in the plague were as great as those of the citizen, and that there had been no considerable loss by emigration. The losses of the slaves in the plague were probably higher in proportion than those of the free (cf. above, p. 7, n. 1).

To the totals of slaves should be added a quite uncertain number of slave children.

(9) The figure 11,000 for the hoplites is based on the army figures of the Corinthian and Theban Wars, and on the assumption that Athens was not then in a condition to put in the field so large a proportion of her nominal hoplite strength as in 431. It may still be too low.

Dion. Hal. *Lys.* p. 526 (= Lys. *Or.* 34 *hyp.*) suggests that there were only 5000 thetes in 400 : for a proposal was made to confine the franchise to possessors of land, and Dionysius says that by this 5000 would be disfranchised. This is not credible. Large numbers of Athenian cleruchs had been driven home after the Peloponnesian War, and though some may have succeeded to land in Attica left vacant by the deaths of former owners, most must have been propertyless. Contrast the number (22,000) disfranchised in 322 (see above, p. 18). I suspect that this figure 5000 is due to a confusion with the 5000 " best " citizens, to whom political power, in the view of Athenian oligarchs, should have been confined.

We cannot estimate the true number. The figure in the table is given only to suggest the great losses this class must have suffered between 415 and 404, but which will to some extent have been made up by impoverishment of hoplites and return of landless cleruchs ; and the consequent change in the relative positions of the hoplites and thetes.

Even if the figures for the men of 18—59 at this time is approximately correct, there is still much room for error in the figure for the total of citizens. At the present time, one at first sight surprising result of the late war is an increase in the proportion of men of 18—59 to the whole population (see below, note C) ; but this is due to the very marked decrease in the birth-rate during the war and hence of the numbers of persons at present living of 0—19 years. The conditions of the Peloponnesian War were so different that we must not assume like results. We only know that there was a noticeable excess of women over men (Xen. *Mem.* ii 2—6).

(10) There must have been far fewer of both metics and slaves in 400 than in 425 ; but it is useless to guess at the numbers.

(11) Only a guess, on the assumption that there were more metics in 338—322 than in 313. There may well have been some thousands more, and correspondingly fewer industrial slaves. As to the latter, all we can say is that there is some evidence that suggests an increase in the use of slaves in industry between 430 and 330 : see below, p. 40.

(12) We are given the total (21,000) of men between 18—59 ; I have divided it between hoplites and thetes on the basis of a much greater decline among the latter following the disfranchisement and emigration in 321.

As stated above, in this table I regard the figures for citizens and metics, in general, as *minima*, those for slaves as *maxima*. Assuming that the figures for the total population of Attica are approximately correct, we are most at sea in estimating the relative proportions of poor citizens (thetes), poor metics and industrial slaves ; that is, we do not kmow at all to what extent slaves dominated the ordinary labour market, how many free men were propertyless men working for a wage, and how many of these free were citizens. And this is a vital question.

On the basis of the figures in this table we would have, to answer some of the questions raised in the beginning of the chapter, the approximate figures of Table II (based on modern populations — see below, p. 75 ff.) for the epheboi (those reaching the age of 18—hoplite census only), for men eligible for the boule (ages 30 and 40— all citizens), and for diaitetai (age 59—hoplite census only).

NOTES TO TABLE II, p. 29.

(1) France (·8) with the lowest percentage, Bulgaria (·96) with the highest.

(2) Greece and Italy with the lowest, Belgium with the highest.

(3) and (4) Bulgaria with the lowest, France with the highest.

(5) The population with full citizen rights only (9000 voters of all ages), after the establishment of the oligarchy. As Ferguson observes (*Hellenistic Athens*, pp. 25–6), the democratic system of rotation of offices, by which no one could hold an office for more than one year, except membership of the boule, and that for two years only, became unworkable with only 9000 citizens with full rights.

(F) 1. In 329 B.C. the corn-production of Attica amounted to 28,500 medimni of wheat and 340,350 medimni of barley, say 370,000 medimni in all.[1] From

---

[1] Inscription found at Eleusis giving the amounts of the first-fruits sent in from Attica (from each of the phylae and some outlying districts) and the colonies of Lemnos, Imbros, and Scyros: *I. G.* ii² 1672. For the exact figures see Kunst, *Berl. Phil. Woch.* 1919, 496 ff ; and Jardé, pp. 31–2, 36 ff. How accurate the ancient calculations were, we cannot say.

This calculation assumes too that the quota sent as firstfruits in 329 was the same (1/600 of barley, 1/1200 of wheat) as that laid down in the law of 418 (*I. G.* i² 76), which, though highly probable, is still not certain. That some alterations were made in the arrangements is shown by *I. G.* ii² 140, a resolution of the Nomothetai of 353/2, amending an earlier law, which must itself have been an amendment of the

TABLE II

Date.	Total Citizen Population. (Modern percentages)	Total Hoplite Population. (Modern percentages)	Males reaching age of			
			18 (·8—·96%)[1]	30 (·64—·78%)[2]	40 (·49—·68%)[3]	59 (·3—·45%)[4]
430	140,000 ?	60,000 ?	480—580	900—1100	700—950	200—260
431	172,000	100,000	800—950	1100—1340	840—1150	330—400
400	90,000 ?	44,000 ?	380—450	560—680	430—580	150—190
323	112,000	58,000	465—570	720—870	550—760	190—230
321[5]	33,000	—	—	230—280	180—250	—
313	84,000	48,000	380—470	540—650	410—570	160—190

this we must deduct one-sixth for seed, and we have
c. 310,000 medimni for consumption. Unfortunately we
have figures for this year only and no means of knowing
if it was an average yield or more or less than the average
—an important matter in Greece where the yield of corn
may vary widely from year to year, more than in northern
Europe.[1] It has been argued indeed that as the years
329—326 were marked by a scarcity of corn and high
prices, this Attic yield is probably below the average.
But this is unsound. The price of corn in Attica was

general law. But ii[2] 140, as ii[2] 1672, shows as well that these changes
were only in the administration, not in the amounts collected nor their
use. For example, the principal difference between the law of 418 and
the practice of 329/8 is that in the former it is enacted that the demarchs
shall collect the quotas each in his own deme, and that the amounts
collected shall be recorded by demes, whereas in the latter the amounts
are recorded by phylae. This may well have been one of the changes
authorised by the law of 353/2 (or, as Elter argues in his very able dissertation on this inscription, by the law which it amended); for it is
there stated that in future the demos is to have full power to decide
the manner of collection. The other important change introduced by
the new law was that henceforth the boule by its representatives (ten
hieropoioi appointed *ad hoc* each year) was to manage the sacrifices
" on behalf of the people of Athens," which it was the chief function of
the *aparche* to provide. (For ii[2] 140, see also Rabes' dissertation, which
I only know through reviews, by Bannier in *Phil. Woch.* xlvi 93, and
by Kern, in *Gnomon* iii 175.)

Koerte's date, 418 B.C. for *I. G.* i[2] 76 seems certain, unless Elter is
right in his view that the *aparche* had nothing to do with the Mysteries
or any other ceremonies at Eleusis, and was applied only to a sacrifice
" on behalf of the people of Athens " and a dedication ; in which case
the *traditiones epistatarum* of 422–19 and of 408/7 (*I. G.* i[2] 311, 313–4)
have equally nothing to do with the law, i[2] 76. But Elter's view, though
well argued, can hardly be maintained : he says that in the sentence
κελευέτω δὲ ὁ ἱεροφάντης καὶ ὁ δαιδοῦχος μυστηρίοις ἀπάρχεσθαι τοὺς ῞Ελληνας,
μυστηρίοις must be taken with κελευέτω, not with ἀπάρχεσθαι, " they
shall announce at the Mysteries," not " to send firstfruits for the Mysteries " ; and this is probably right. But I find it hard to believe that
even Athens at her most arrogant would have invited the rest of Greece,
however politely, to contribute to a sacrifice which was only to be on
behalf of herself.

Bannier's doubts (*Berl. Phil. Woch.* 1915, p. 1232) as to whether
i[2] 76 is at all a general law regulating the future collection and use of the
aparche, are quite groundless.

[1] The following figures give the yield of wheat and barley per
hectare and the amount of land sown in 1922 and 1923 for the five most
productive provinces of Greece proper (publication of the Ministry of
National Economy for 1923 : they are however admittedly not based
on a scientific survey, but on returns sent in by small local authorities).
It will be observed how wide the variations can be, in the area sown,
the yield per hectare, and in the price. (Attica, Boeotia and the Megarid
form one province ; there are no figures for Attica alone. Laconia and
Messenia practically comprise the territory of ancient Sparta before

determined not by the home yield, but by the supplies
from abroad, as much as in England (even more, for the
corn that mattered was wheat, whereas the home pro-
duct was mostly barley) ; if anything a general scarcity
and high prices would cause a greater production in
Attica, and we hear in fact, just about this time, com-
plaints (from a mine-owner) of the losses of mine-owners
and the exorbitant gains of agriculture.[1]

the emancipation of Messene ; Larissa and Trikkala together correspond
roughly to Thessaly.)

		WHEAT.			BARLEY.		
		Area sown (hectares)	*Yield per hectare.*	*Price per metric quintal.*	*Area sown (hec-tares).*	*Yield per hectare.*	*Price per metric quintal.*
Attica-Boeotia	1922	59,725	350 kg.	228 dr.	9,225	650 kg.	174 dr.
	1923	45,077	290 kg.	390 dr.	4,575	660 kg.	351 dr.
Laconia	1922	6,611	560 kg.	125 dr.	2,294	590 kg.	109 dr.
	1923	7,852	770 kg.	358 dr.	2,357	700 kg.	244 dr.
Messenia	1922	12,691	710 kg.	245 dr.	1,416	690 kg.	180 dr.
	1923	12,271	730 kg.	399 dr.	1,443	770 kg.	288 dr.
Larissa	192:	64,965	400 kg.	234 dr.	13,466	640 kg.	164 dr.
	1923	71,803	400 kg.	300 dr.	18,118	520 kg.	210 dr.
Trikkala	1922	23,163	350 kg.	278 dr.	3,174	270 kg.	186 dr.
	1923	31,110	560 kg.	281 dr.	3,635	610 kg.	195 dr.

The total area of land under crops in Attica-Boeotia varied in the
eight years 1916—1923 between 72,650 ha. in 1921 (wheat 27,492 ha.,
barley 6019 ha.) and 125,803 ha. in 1923, with an average of 102,085 ha.
(average under wheat 39,709, under barley 8959 ha.). There are similar
fluctuations in the figures for the other provinces. They are due in
part to political conditions. (I am indebted to the staff of the Greek
Legation in London for the opportunity to examine these and other
statistics of modern Greece, and I desire to record my grateful acknow-
ledgements.) The fluctuations in the prices are largely due to the fall
in the value of the drachma ; but they are not consistent in all the
provinces.

[1] Dem. xlii 20–21, 31. See also Jardé, pp. 46 7, who points out

2. According to Demosthenes (xx 31—2) the import of corn from the kingdom of Bosporus into Piraeus, in 355, was 400,000 medimni, and this equalled the import from all other countries. Demosthenes was a politician, and so was probably not speaking the truth ; he wishes to emphasize the importance of the Bosporus to Athens ; but whether he is exaggerating the true amount of imports from the Bosporus or only their proportion to those from elsewhere we do not know. In the former case the total of imports will be less, in the latter more than 800,000 medimni. As he professes to quote official figures for the Bosporus, we may believe these and safely assume a greater amount than 400,000 medimni from all other countries : say twice as much.

Demosthenes' actual figures and the Eleusis inscription give us c. 1,100,000 medimni per annum for consumption in Attica. At an average of 6 medimni per head (1 choinix a day = $7\frac{1}{2}$ medimni a year, was the regular allowance for grown men[1] ; allow two-thirds of this for women and children) this was food for a population of less than 200,000. If we admit another 100,000 medimni for the average harvest of Attica (something may be allowed for an under-assessment of the harvest, to keep the quota as low as possible), and suppose that the corn from Russia was only one half of and not equal to the corn imported from other countries (and these are extremes, and we are ignoring all the barley needed for animal consumption[2]), we have a total of 1,600,000 medimni or sufficient for about 270,000 persons, or rather less ; for the majority of the slave population were grown men and should have consumed $7\frac{1}{2}$ medimni a year each. Thus :

that our figures belong to the harvest of 329, and must not be applied to a vague " period " of short supplies, unless this year is expressly included.

[1] Of wheat ; more if barley-bread was eaten. But all imported corn was wheat.

[2] Jardé, pp. 126–7, reckons that animals consumed about 300,000 medimni of barley a year, about as much as the Attic harvest of 329. It was in any case a very considerable amount.

(1) Production of Attica
  (for consumption) 310,000 medimni
   add   100,000 ,,

(2) Import
  (a) from Bosporus 400,000 ,,
  (b) from elsewhere
  2 × 400,000 800,000 ,,

       1,610,000

at 6 medimni per head, c. 270,000 portions.

These figures are of the roughest, but they show that, on the available evidence, for the period 360—320 we cannot allow a population of more than 250—275,000. Actually with the population for 338—322 (258,000) distributed as suggested in the table on p. 26, and ignoring foreigners temporarily resident,[1] Athens would have required about 1,500,000 medimni yearly; had there been 150,000 male slaves (on the evidence of Hypereides), but no more women slaves, over 2,000,000 medimni would have been required, and had there been 400,000 (on the evidence of Ctesicles) about 3,700,000. It is clear that these figures must be rejected. Equally we must remember that this figure for corn consumption serves only as a check on our population figures, showing that they are near the maximum, not that they are exact.

It is very unsatisfactory having to deal with evidence so limited in quantity and so wanting in precision, and of this little having to emend or neglect part. Those who have worked at it know best how unsatisfactory it is. The proper use of statistics (or rather one of them) is to check generalisations[2]; we not only cannot often

---

[1] And ignoring also all slave-children, born in Attica. But we have no means of learning how many there were. There were some children among the manumitted slaves (see below, p. 42). Ignoring also animal consumption.

[2] I will give an instance of one of them. On the strength of Xenophon's *Oeconomicus* it is commonly said that the usual age of

do that, but even at times have to do the opposite—use generalizations to check the statistics ; and at best have only the roundest of round numbers for examining even so primary a question as that of the relative numbers of slave and free. Those accustomed to deal with modern statistics, with their precision and amplitude of detail, may exclaim at the impossibility of doing anything with material so inadequate. But it is a question of historical judgment—how to use the evidence we have. Because a task is difficult and needs delicate handling is no reason for shirking it ; and, if the above analysis of the evidence is correct, we have something—chiefly because that evidence, such as it is, is of sufficient variety that one kind can be used to check another. It is of value if it is established as highly probable, first that the citizen population in 431 was nearer 50,000 than 30,000, and a hundred years later nearer 40,000 than 20,000 ; and, second, that the number of slaves was at no time larger than 100–120,000. It is of the greatest importance if we have established that there was a considerable natural increase of the population between 480 and 430, and between 400 and 320 ; for periods of growth in population have been rare throughout recorded history, and are due to special causes. We must remember, in addition to the figures given in the table on p. 26, the considerable emigration of citizens in cleruchies between 480 and 430 ; and, for Greece in general, the great expansion of population, for two generations at least, after 320, implied by the colonization of Western Asia.

Lastly, in so important a matter as this, it is essential to know both the extent and the limits of our evidence. As Prof. Nillson says of his own subject : " it is the habit of mathematicians either to solve a problem or to demonstrate that it is insoluble. So too this problem ought not to be put aside, but must be subjected to a

marriage for girls was 15. The same, or something similar, is asserted of modern Greece ; but in the latter case we have statistics, which tell us that the proportion of girls under 20 who are married is from 1.5 to 2.7% (varying in different districts) of the whole number under 20, rather lower than in this country.

seàrching analysis in order to discover how far it can be solved, and how far it is insoluble : for in historical research the partial clearing up of a problem is the general issue, and the mere stating of the limits of a problem is a step forward."[1] Besides, there is a chance of fresh evidence turning up : one hope that the new excavations of Athens will give results good enough to compensate for the damage to the modern town lies in the discovery of new inscriptions, among which may well be more lists of epheboi and bouleutai, and of manumitted slaves, and building accounts—inscriptions of the kind that have already thrown vivid if scattered light on ancient Athens. The new evidence should fit easily into its place, if the analysis of existing evidence has been properly done.

[1] *Minoan-Mycenean Religion*, p. 4.

II

COUNTRY AND TOWN POPULATION

WE have no figures at all to show movement of the population of Attica between the country and the town. But we have certain other evidence, and since this is valuable as far as it goes, and it is better to be clear as to what the evidence is than simply to assume a movement from the country to the town, I will briefly state it.

At the time of Cleisthenes, to judge by the figures of bouleutai,[1] the population of the town-demes was rather less than one-third of the total citizen population (rather more, probably, than two-sevenths). It must be remembered that these town-demes were not necessarly urban in character ; many, perhaps the majority, were rural, the town trittys comprising land as far west as Mt. Aigaleos, and much agricultural land N. and E. of Athens (to the foot of Hymettos at least), and between Athens and Phaleron. What the *urban* population was we can only guess from the number of bouleutai representing certainly urban demes, Kerameis, Kydathenaieis, Skambonidai, Melite, Phaleron, and Peiraeus : perhaps 65—70 in all, or not more than one-seventh of the whole[2] ; or, if Alopeke and Kollytos were already urban, as they certainly soon became to judge from the number of metics who lived in them, then about one-sixth of the whole.

1. It is well-known that most of the noble families of Athens belonged to town-demes (or at least such as were prominent in public affairs). Amongst them were Megacles and most of the Alcmaeonidae, Aristeides, Euryptolemus cousin to Pericles, Thucydides son of

---

[1] See below, p. 66.

[2] See below, pp. 56 ff. It seems probable that the many very small demes in the town-trittys were originally rural in character ; there seems to be no reason why an urban population should have been divided up so minutely by Cleisthenes.

For some demes whose trittys is uncertain (by which the figures in this section are slightly affected), see below, pp. 56 ff.

Melesias, all of Alopeke ; Leobotes son of Alcmeon, of
Agryle ; Callias and Hipponicus of Ankyle ; Thucydides
son of Olorus, of Halimus; Strombichides, of Euonymeis;
Glaucon and Leagros, beloved of the potters, of Kerameis
the potters' deme ; Hipparchus son of Charmus, and
Plato's family, of Kollytos ; Sophocles of Kolonos ;
Andocides and Teisandros (hence also Isagoras ?),
Kydathenaieis ; Miltiades and Cimon, Lakiadai ; Alci-
biades and his friend Adeimantus son of Leucolophides,
Skambonidai ; Xanthippus and Pericles, of Cholargos.[1]
Others who, if not noble, were prominent in the fifth
century are Cleon (who was not one of the new rich :
his father had been choregos in 467) and Aristophanes,
both of Kydathene, Socrates, Hyperbolus, Lamachus ;
and all the Hermokopidai we know of, except one.[2] On
the other hand, comparatively few public men in the
fifth century came from the inland or the coast : Calli-
machus the polemarch from Aphidna,[3] Themistocles of
Phrearrioi, the *novus homo*, who married into a town-
deme (his father-in-law was of Alopeke), Nicias Kydan-
tides (each of these two characteristic in his own way),
Laches of Aixone, Phormion, who was perhaps from
Paiania, Demosthenes from Aphidna[4] ; other prominent
men were Aeschylus (Eleusis) and Euripides (Phlya),
and several of those in the oligarchic movement—Anti-
phon (Rhamnus), Peisander (Acharnae), Phrynichus
(Deiradiotes), and Theramenes (Steiria) ; the demes of

[1] If Cholargos was a town-deme : see below, p. 60, n. 2. It was
at any rate in the plain of Athens, and not distant from the centre.
Cf. Bekker, *Anecd.* 257 (quoted by Wade-Gery, *C. Q.* 1931, p. 77.1) :
Εὐπατρίδαι ἐκαλοῦντο οἱ αὐτὸ τὸ ἄστυ οἰκοῦντες. The use of ἀστοί to mean
citizens, evidently the older use, points in the same direction.

[2] Another was very likely Phaenippus, archon on the year of
Marathon ; who probably belonged to the family of Callias (cf. Hdt.
vi. 121, Macan ad loc.) : very anti-tyrannical and perhaps personal
enemies of the Alcmeonids ; cf. Callias, Cimon's brother-in-law.
Xanthippus, archon in 479/8, may well have been of Pericles'
family, and of Cholargos.

[3] The backwoodsmen Harmodius and Aristogeiton were also from
Aphidna.

[4] There was a Θουκυδίδης Ἀλκισθένους Ἀφιδναῖος active between
340 and 320, certainly related to the general (*P. A.* 7270) ; and his
name suggests that there was a family connexion between the general
and the historian.

Cleophon and Critias are not known. Towards the end of the century, and in the earlier years of the fourth, Thrasybulus and Agyrrius, both of Kollytos,[1] belong to the town-district ; the other Thrasybulus (Steiria) and Conon (Anaphlystos) to the coast.[2] But in the fourth century there is a very great difference : very few public men from the town—Lycurgus (Boutadai), Hypereides (Kollytos), Demetrius (Phaleron) ; and large numbers from inland and the coast, Timotheus, Iphicrates, and Chabrias; Callistratus, Androtion, Chares, Demosthenes, Demades, Aeschines, Pythocles, and Meidias ; Eubulus, Hegesippus, Polyeuctus, and many others.[3] This is not due to the rise of a country party ; but to the fact that many families had moved from the country into the town.[4]

2. From the Erechtheum building inscriptions (*I.G.* i[2] 373–4 : 409–7 B.C.) we have the names of 22 citizen skilled workers whose demes we know : 15 come from town-demes, 7 from inland. The latter were probably already settled in Athens, or at least worked there for some years. Some forty metic workers are known, all of town-demes. On the small fragments dealing with the rebuilding of the Piraeus walls in 395–4 (*I.G.* ii[2] 1657–64) we have six citizens, 2 from the town, 2 from

---

[1] Plato and Agyrrius make as interesting a pair from Kollytos as Cleon and Aristophanes from Kydathene.

[2] It is perhaps worth noting that Themistocles, Conon and Chabrias, all definitely connected with the navy rather than the army, come from coast demes. There is no evidence to show that Athenian sailors came mainly from the coast demes. But the populousness of the coastal district between Peiraeus and Sunium, and between Thorikos and Oropos, as shown by the large demes Aixone, Halai, Anaphlystos, Anagyrasioi, Myrrhinus, Marathon and Rhamnus, is the greatest contrast in distribution of population between ancient and modern Attica (at least before the very rapid increase of Athens and Piraeus in the last 15 years) ; and they may have been largely sailors and fishermen.

[3] Phocion's deme is not known. (His house was in Melite.)

[4] Demosthenes, for example, was certainly born in Athens. Timotheus had a house in Peiraeus (Dem. xlix 22). Phrynichus, on the other hand, in the fifth century, was born in his country-deme (Deiradiotai, near Thorikos), and came to Athens for politics ; unlike his honest fellow-demesman Polystratos, who, says Lysias, being of a well-to-do family, came to Athens as a boy to be educated, and went back to his deme and worked his land (Lys. xx 11—12)

the coast, 2 from inland.[1]   From the Eleusis building
inscriptions (356 and 330–26 B.C. : *I.G.* ii² 1666, 1670–5)
we have some 36 citizens whose demes are known, 21
from town-demes, 15 from the coast and inland. All
except one are contractors for building or transport, or
merchants, not workers.[2]   There were rather more
metic workers,. contractors and merchants employed
than citizens (and twenty-one foreign merchants). One
of the citizens was from Eleusis itself, one from neigh-
bouring Thria ; of the metics all lived in Athens or
Peiraeus, except seven who lived in Eleusis. Here again
it is reasonable to suppose that the citizens belonging
to inland and coast demes were settled in the town-area,
like the metics. Scherling's view that we can discover
the distribution of industry in Attica from the demes of
citizen-workers as well as of metics is quite untenable.[3]
His own figures, from the inscriptions only, are sufficient
to disprove it : 50 citizens from town-demes, 22 from the
coast, 34 from inland—craftsmen, contractors and merchants. Metics—210 from town-demes, 12 from the
coast (all but one from Eleusis or the mining-district),
6 from inland. The reason why the metics settled in the
towns to trade is obvious ; is it likely that the citizens
ignored these advantages ? [4]

[1] All contractors, not workers, and all for very small contracts.
We have also the names of one more citizen of unknown deme, and two
foreigners, but no metics ; the foreigners perhaps refugees. Significant
of changed conditions after the Peloponnesian War ?

[2] Zimmern's view (*Solon and Croesus*, p. 146) that we can trace
from the Erechtheum and Eleusis inscriptions a decline in the use of
slave labour, is the reverse of the truth. There are 15 slaves known as
having worked on the former, all skilled craftsmen, individuals! at least
71 at Eleusis, all the servants of contractors. The chief difference between
the two sets of inscriptions is that on the Erechtheum work was let out
individually to skilled men, citizen, metic or slave (only some of the unskilled work being done by a contractor with his own men), at Eleusis it
was mostly let out to small contractors, many of them with slaves.

[3] There does seem to have been some predominance—natural
enough— of stone-workers from the demes near Pentelicus and Hy-
mettus (Scherling, pp. 52–3.)

[4] In the same way we should be cautious of assuming a revival
of the mesogeia towards the end of the third century from the predominance of men from demes in that district in *I. G.* ii² 791, the list of
subscriptions for the state's need in 232 B.C., as do Jardé, p. 163 and
Ferguson, *Hellenistic Athens*, pp. 204–7. Families may have been long
divorced from their demes by that time.

Similarly, if we examine the demes of the many citizen merchants and capitalists, and others who take part as guarantors or witnesses of contracts made in Athens or Peiraeus, to be found in the *Private Speeches* of the fourth century, we observe the same phenomenon : these essentially urban activities belong as much to men of inland and coastal demes as to those of the town demes, to men, that is, whose families, most of them, had settled in the towns, as Demosthenes, who lived over his furniture factory in Athens, as Komon of Halai, whose sail-factory at Peiraeus was also his home (Dem. xlviii 12). Similarly, in Athens, as everywhere, successful men from the town would buy estates in the country, as Pasion the banker in three separate demes, one of them presumably Acharnai which he chose as his deme.[1]

3. Further evidence of a similar kind is to be got from the manumission inscriptions (*I.G.* ii[2] 1553—1578), all of which belong to the period 340—320.[2] They give us the name and deme of the ex-master, and the deme and occupation of the ex-slave.[3] From these we can get the following figures :

[1] Dem. xxxv is as good an example as any to show the part played by citizens in trade, and the way in which men of country-demes lived in the town. The subject of the dispute is a bottomry loan made by an Athenian, of Sphettos (introduced by two friends of his, also of Sphettos) to a merchant originally of Phaselis. Witnesses are from Leukonoe and Peiraeus, Pitheis and Anagyrasioi (as well as a Boeotian and an ἰσοτελής). Witnesses to various actions subsequent to the original transaction include the navigator of the ship, and travellers on it, men from Acharnai, Hestiaieis, Xypete, Cholleidai, Aphidna, Thymaitadai, and Thria, besides two men of Halicarnassus.

[2] On 1578 we have part of the title preserved, with a reference to δίκαι ἀποστασίου held before the Polemarch (for the freedmen became at once metics) on 15th Hekatombaion (the same day as that for manumissions at Chaeroneia, as observed by Drachmann). On the stone on which most names are preserved (1570), both sides of the stone had been inscribed (as on many others), there are 36 names on one side, and these are not all that had been originally inscribed. Hence we can assume a minimum of 50, and perhaps this is near the average number manumitted (by this process) every year. The number, and the fact that all the δίκαι were held on the same day, show that they were a pure formality, held for the purpose of officially recording the men's freedom : the ex-slave left his master, the latter claimed him formally, the jury decided for the slave.

[3] The occupations of the metics enfranchised in 403 (*I. G.* ii[2] 10) are also recorded.

1. Ex-slaves : men   142 (incl. 7 boys).
    women 111 (incl. 10 girls).
2. Ex-masters : citizens 203[1]
    metics 23
    foreigners 9 (all domiciled in Attica)[2]
    ἔρανοι 16
3. Ex-slaves : deme (and therefore domicile)
    Athens and environs   125
    Peiraeus   45
    Coast and inland   15[3]
4. Metic masters : deme and domicile
    Athens and environs   14
    Peiraeus   2
    Coast and inland   0
5. Citizen masters : deme
    Town   60
    Coast   32
    Inland   59
6. Occupations of ex-slaves :

	Agricul-ture.	Manu-facture.	Trans-port.	Distri-butive.	Mis-cell.[4]	None.[5]	Total.
Men	12	26[6]	10[7]	21[8]	10	36	115
Women	0	48[9]	0	7[8]	1	21	77

[1] Or 188 ; 15 come from an inscription (1575) which may not belong to the manumission series.

[2] 2 πρόξενοι, 2 Olynthians, 1 Theban, 1 Troezenian, 1 Plataean (all ἰσοτελεῖς or ἰσοπολῖται), and 2 δημόσιοι, public slaves who manumit their own slaves.

[3] Including 4 in the mining district, 5 in Salamis.

[4] Clerks, money-lenders, cooks, barbers, and general labourers (μισθωτοί).

[5] Those to whose name no occupation is attached are probably old men and women retired from active work with their savings or a pension ; most of them domestic servants. Where the occupation is given, it should be descriptive of the trade proposed to be taken, not simply of past activity ; just as with the metics of 403.

[6] Including one miner, the only one released from this the hardest and cruellest of ancient industries ; and he may have been engaged in the smelting works, not a hewer working underground.

[7] Some owners of animals, the rest porters.

[8] 10 merchants and general shopkeepers, 11 specialized (ἀρτοπῶλαι, &c.), among the men ; 3 general, 4 specialized, among the women.

[9] 44 of them textile workers (ταλασιουργοί), who had as slaves presumably worked at home, not in factories ; the other 4 were 1 ἀκεστρία, 1 κιθαρῳδός, 2 cobblers.

If we now combine where possible (that is, where we have both pieces of information) tables 5 and 6 above, we get the following :—

7. Demes of citizen masters divided according to the occupation of their ex-slaves—

	Agricul- ture.	Manu- facture.	Trans- port.	Dis- tribu- tive.	Misc.	Total.
Town-demes						
Men	1	10	1	3	6	21
Women	—	8	—	2	2	12
Coast-demes						
Men	0	2	3	4	0	9
Women	—	8	—	1	0	9
Inland demes						
Men	5	4	3	3	1	16
Women	—	8	—	1	1	10

It will be seen that whereas more masters of ex-slaves who have urban occupations (manufacturers, distributors and porters, and most of the miscellaneous) belong to the town-district than to either of the other two districts, those belonging to these two combined are in a majority ; and when we add to that, the fact that all the metic masters and nearly all the ex-slaves,[1] lived in town-demes, it is right to assume that the majority of citizen masters belonging to inland and coast demes were living in Athens or Peiraeus.

4. The evidence from dicasts' tickets (*I.G.* ii² 1835—1923) is hardly sufficient to help us ; we have so few. But, bearing in mind the fact that the majority of dicasts

---

[1] It is noteworthy that of the known domiciles of the few ex-slaves engaged in agriculture, 5 are in the town area (Oa, Iphistiadai, Kollytos, Skambonidai and Phaleron), only 2 in the country (Hagnous and Salamis). It must be repeated that a large part of the town area remained agricultural, suitable especially for market-gardeners.

In the cases where the *domicile* both of the ex-masters (the metics) and ex-slaves is known, 7 of the latter enter their former master's deme, 4—6 enter a different one. In one case two ex-slaves freed by the same man enter each a different deme.

must have come from near Athens, I give the figures for
what they are worth :

Town-demes   17
Coast-demes   19
Inland-demes   20

Some of the last two groups naturally come from the
demes nearer to Athens, as Acharnai and Aixone.

5. The tombstones of the fourth and third centuries
found in Athens and Peiraeus (*I.G.* ii 1682 ff.) tell the same
story.[1]   There is scarcely a deme, however small and
remote, that is not represented among the tombstones
found in Athens and Peiraeus and the near environs ;
the larger country and coast-demes are well-represented
—almost as well as the town-demes.   In almost all cases,
the existence of tombs means that the family had settled
there.   From the nature of the case this does not give
us any statistics of migrations ; but we can be certain
of a considerable movement to the town.

Here are some characteristic figures for a few demes[2]—
compiled from *I.G.* :—

A. TOWN-DEMES.

	Total known.	Found in or near Athens or Peiraeus.	Found elsewhere in Attica.	Provenance not given.
Ankyle	7	4	0	3
Halimous	5	3	0	2
Alopeke	20	9	0	11
Euonymeis	27	14	0	13
Iphistiadai	5	3	1	1
Kerameis	23	13	0	10
Kydathenaieis	24	12	0	12
Kytherrioi	4	3	0	1
Lakiadai	20	11	0	9
Leukonoeis	23	14	6	3
Meliteis	20	12	1	7
Peiraieis	23	9	3	9
Skambonidai	11	8	1	2

[1] Not many tombstones of citizens of the fifth century or earlier
exist (*I. G.* i² 970—1086) ; and hardly any of these have the *demotica*
added.

[2] For the relative sizes of demes, see the tables given below, pp. 56 ff.

B. COAST AND INLAND-DEMES.

	Total known.	Found near site of deme.	Found in or near Athens or Peiraeus.	Found elsewhere.	Provenance not given.
Angeleis	6	0	6	0	0
Hagnousioi	12	0	5	0	7
Athmoneis	17	4	6	2	5
Aigilieis	17	0	13	0	4
Aixoneis	34	2	23	1	8
Halaieis	36	6	18	3	9
Amphitropaieis	6	0	4	0	2
Anakaieis	4	0	3	0	1
Aphidnaioi	28	0	20	0	8
Acharneis	51	11	22	2	16
Dekeleeis	7	4	1	0	2
Eleusinioi	13	2	3	4	4
Thorikioi	18	0	16	0	2
Kephaleis	20	9	7	1	3
Kephisieis	20	8	8	0	4
Kropidai	3	1	1	0	1
Kydantidai	8	0	7	0	1
Marathonioi	14	0	7	1	6
Paianieis	25	7	10	1	7
Plotheis	5	0	3	0	2
Prospaltioi	10	2	6	0	2
Sounieis	20	5	9	0	6
Teithrasioi	3	0	3	0	0

These figures illustrate (and it is all that they do) the migration from the country to the town.[1]

6. There is other evidence which illustrates, not the growth of the urban population, but a general movement from place to place in Attica. In the various inscriptions dealing with leases, mortgages and sales of land or houses (including sequestrations by the state) (*I.G.* i²,

[1] This must not however be exaggerated; there is plenty of evidence in Demosthenes and Isaeus that men continued to live in the country and cultivate the land; and the figures for the corn-production of Attica in 329 (above, p. 28) show that the land was well-cultivated, especially when we remember that the vine and the olive, not wheat and barley, are the principal products of Attica.

325—332, 905 ; ii² 2495—2768), it is rare to find a man owning or leasing property in his own deme, comparatively common to find the reverse. Similarly the owners of mines and smelting works in the Laurion district come from all over Attica—of those known, 24 from inland-demes, 13 from the town, 18 from coast-demes ; and of these last only 12 are from demes in or near the mining district. They would not necessarily be settled in the district ; but they will have had to spend much time there.

When therefore Demosthenes states that in the middle of the fourth century the majority of Halimousioi lived in their deme[1] (which was in the town district, but on its S.E. border, not urban in character), and when Xenophon implies that large numbers at least of Eleusinioi and Aixoneis lived in their demes at the end of the fifth century,[2] we must at the same time keep in mind all this other evidence. Thucydides says in a well-known passage that most Athenians continued to live in the country long after the synoecism, right up to the beginning of the Peloponnesian War ; he is contrasting Athens implicitly with some other states (perhaps Corinth and Argos), and with what would have been expected from the centralization of government—particularly after Cleisthenes, when each of the ten phylae had its centre and meeting-place in Athens. We know as well that many of the old unities survived the formation of the new demes and phylae—mesogeioi, trikomoi, tetrapoleis, and the like—and that there were a number of local cults and festivals independent of the town.[3] Yet many citizens must have been migrating to Athens during the fifth century ; and many more must have been settled there in the fourth. In addition to these, practically all the metics (of the 270 or so whose deme is known, fewer than 30 are from the country—these

---

[1] lvii 10. It was 8 miles or so from Athens, and the meeting of demesmen was held in Athens.

[2] *Hell.* ii 4. 8—9, 26.

[3] Solders, *Die ausserstädtischen Kulte.*

mostly from Eleusis, Salamis and the mining-district), and nearly all the industrial slaves except the miners lived in the town. We may assume, I think, rather over a third of the citizen population, say 60,000, to have been living in the town-area by 430, nearly a half, say 50,000 a hundred years later ; and therefore the same proportion of domestic slaves. On the basis of the figures given in the table on p. 26 we would have for the population of Athens and Peiraeus and environs :

In 430 : citizens   60000
       metics   25000
       slaves : domestic 25000 (belonging to citizens)
                     10000 (belonging to metics)
         industrial 35000

               155000

In 330 : citizens   50000
       metics   36000
       slaves : domestic 20000 (belonging to citizens)
                     12000 (belonging to metics)
         industrial 50000

               168000[1]

In addition, a considerable floating population of foreigners, especially sailors in merchant vessels, and rowers in the fleet. That is, in 430 over half the population of Attica, in 330 nearly three-quarters, concentrated in the town-area : very inexact figures, but probably not far from the truth. And it must be remembered that with the growth of this population, especially through the immigration of metics and industrial slaves, the town-trittys will have become much more urban in character than it was in 500 B.C.

[1] Jardé, p. 196, on the evidence of Xen. *Mem.* iii 6. 14, assumes an urban citizen population of c. 40,000 (in Athens alone) or rather more. But Xenophon, in saying there are "more than 10,000 households" (a purely conventional figure) is referring to the whole state, not to the town of Athens.

Even so, even if the probability of these figures is granted, it must be remembered that we are only at the threshold of useful statistics : only total numbers, a rough distribution between social classes, and between town and country. We still know nothing of the *cause* of the increase of citizen population between 500 and 430 and between 400 and 320 (if there was an increase), that is, whether it was a higher birth-rate or lower death-rate, or both ; we should guess that the latter was the principal cause (as in Europe from the end of the eighteenth century), due to improved economic opportunities and improved medical science. Still less do we know anything of the birth-rate and death-rate of the different classes, of the size of households in the different classes, of housing conditions, of industrial and occupational distribution ; we can only guess at the size of some industrial groups, we do not know the average nor the commonest type. That is, we cannot even attempt (and perhaps never shall be able to attempt) a tithe of a true *Social Structure of Athens*, such as is done for modern countries.[1]

[1] Cf. Carr-Saunders and Jones, *Social Structure of England and Wales, as illustrated by statistics* (Oxford, 1927).

NOTE A

THE VALUE OF ATHENIAN STATISTICS. THE BOULEUTAI LISTS

THERE has been much variety in the use made of such statistics as we have, and some discussion as to their value.

The ten phylae were made approximately equal by Cleisthenes, and since they were large units, and a man belonged to his father's phyle (except in the rare cases of adoption outside the phyle), they would remain approximately equal. A phyle might suffer exceptional losses in a war (as Erechtheis in 459–8[1]), but we should expect these to average out in course of time. The organization both of the army and of the Boulê depended on their equality[2]; so, to a less extent, did that of the dicasteria; clerouchoi were selected by phylae[3] (though not in exactly equal numbers); and when a number of Samian democrats were given Athenian citizenship in 405–4, they were to be carefully distributed among the phylae[4]; so were the metics of 403.[5] There was clearly the intention of preserving the equality of the phylae (as well as, perhaps, of avoiding concentration of the new voting power). How far this equality was actually preserved till the end of the fourth century, we have no means of telling. When the two new phylae were created in 307, demes or parts of demes were transferred to them from the old ones; assuming that the adjustment was made in such a way as to make all the twelve phylae equal, and taking as his basis the representation in the boulê of the demes so transferred, Sundwall has concluded

[1] There is no need to suppose the famous inscription to be one of ten similar memorials, one for each phyle; we have no other examples. It was unique, due to the exceptional part played by Erechtheis on these campaigns. (Hondius, *Nov. Att. Inscr.* pp. 118–9, argues that *I.G.* i[2] 933, to which perhaps 937 and 938 belong, is from a similar memorial of another phyle. This is quite uncertain; even the four fragments of 933 may not all belong together, and if they do, may not all refer to one phyle.)

[2] Perhaps of the navy too, if the *trittyum termini* (*I.G.* i[2] 897—901: Hiller ad loc.) found in the Peiraeus have reference to men called up for naval service. But this is doubtful. In the big naval inscription ii[2] 1951 neither the epibatai nor the citizen rowers served by phylae; and though, as can be seeen from the metics and the large number of slaves who served, this was an exceptional occasion (probably Arginusae), in none of the naval casualty lists is there distribution by phylae. (For the attribution of this inscription to Arginusae, see now Kolbe, in *Phil. Woch.* 1932, 35/38 (*Poland-Festschrift*), pp. 83–8).

[3] *I.G.* ii[2] 1952.

[4] *I.G.* ii[2] 1[34].

[5] ii[2] 10 (see *S.E.G.* i, ii & iii).

that Erechtheis (from which demes with formerly 10 bouleutai were transferred), Aigeis (12 bouleutai), Pandionis (12), and Antiochis (11) were approximately equal to each other in 307 and each rather larger than one-tenth of the whole state ; that Leontis (4), Akamantis (5), Oineis (3), and Hippothontis (4) were about equal to each other, and each smaller than one-tenth of the whole ; and that Kekropis (16) was the most populous of the phylae, and Aiantis (from which no demes were transferred) the smallest.[1] This may be roughly true ; but it is assuming that the representation of the demes in the boulê was kept strictly proportional to their populations, which is doubtful.[2] If we had enough names in the *Prosopographia Attica*, we ought to be able to tell approximate size by distribution ; but probably there are still too few, so that exceptional circumstances of discovery may upset the average. The actual distribution of these names is as follows :—

Erechtheis	1312	Oineis	1125
Aigeis	1540	Kekropis	1333
Pandionis	1223	Hippothontis	1077
Leontis	1502	Aiantis	979
Akamantis	1130	Antiochis	1058

which suggests a different position from Sundwall's for Leontis, Kekropis and Antiochis.[3]

The demes are in a different category. There too a man belonged to his father's deme, so that if life had all been smooth, the relative sizes of the demes would have remained much the same in the fifth and fourth centuries. But many of the demes were so small that a catastrophe, like the plague or a disastrous battle, might permanently affect their numbers. Were adjustments regularly made in representation of demes in the boulê (within the phylê ; for the phylê retained its 50 members) to reflect such changes ? There seems to be no

---

[1] *Epigraphische Beiträge*, pp. 88—91 (some of these figures of bouleutai are uncertain).

[2] If we look for instance at the figures in the table given below, p. 59, for Halimous, Leukonoeis and Oion (all in Leontis), that is, those from *P.A.*, the bouleutai of the fourth and of the second century and the epheboi of 326, we should certainly suppose that the first was over-represented and the latter two under-represented in the fourth century, and that this anomaly was later corrected.

[3] Based on Kirchner's lists at the end of *Prosopographia Attica*, with adjustments (see below, p. 56, n. 1) ; therefore excluding all those whose phylae are known, but not their demes.

Cavaignac has also used the *Prosopographia* figures, but for the demes, where they are much more unreliable (see below, p. 53 f.) ; for the phylae, he supposes Aigeis, Pandionis, Leontis and Akamantis to have been much less populous, the rest more populous, to suit his theory of Athenian dispositions at Marathon (*Monde Méd.* 512, 515), forgetting his belief in the *prosopographia* figures.

evidence for it. There may have been an adjustment in 403, when the losses of the war and the return of cleruchs would, one would suppose, have upset the balance of representation ; but we do not hear of any, and unfortunately the only list of bouleutai dating from before Eukleides is so incomplete that it does not furnish a basis for comparison.[1] Within the fourth century we can observe variations of one bouleutes more or less in several demes, but so fragmentary is our evidence that we cannot be certain whether the change is a permanent adjustment or one designed to set right, one year with another, the representation of certain demes.[2] For example, in Aigeis : Bate, 2 c. 350 B.C., 1 in 341–0 and in 336–5 ; Kydantidai, 1 c.

[1] *I.G.* i² 398 (408–7 B.C.), for Erechtheis (see below, p. 55, n. 1) ; nor have we any complete list for Erechtheis of the fourth century with which to make a partial comparison.

[2] The inscriptions which certainly or, in my opinion, very probably, give lists or parts of lists, of bouleutai, are as follows : ii² 1698, 1700, 1740–3, 1745–53, 2377 (?), 2413. 1699 may be another ; but its form is different from the rest, in that the names are not arranged by demes (important for the boule) ; in any case it is of little value for our purposes, as it is only a small part of the whole, and none of the figures for the demes is final. 1697 is not certain, and the figure 6 for Phegaieis (Aigeis) makes it unlikely. 1746 presents a difficulty ; the stone is lost and it is not quite certain that it is a list of bouleutai. In the column preserved we have fragments of five names of an unknown deme said to be Oa by Kirchner on the strength of some very uncertain identifications, then some more demes of Oineis with figures corresponding to those of No. 1745 (the complete list of Oineis). On the previous column, as printed in *I.G.*, there had been 6 (+ ?) names of one deme, 9 of a second (there is then a gap of at least 8 lines) ; if this column also belongs to Oineis, this second deme would be Thriasioi, which had 7 bouleutai only a few years earlier (No. 1745). It would be better to assume the 6 of the first column to be of Oa (as on 1745), and the 9 *plus* the 8 in the gap *plus* the 5 at the beginning of col. 2 to be the 22 Acharneis (as 1745) ; assuming, that is, that there were originally no more than these 5 names at the head of this column (the top of the stone is missing). In No. 1698, besides some names from Hippothontis and Oineis, there is a group of 17 names of an unknown deme, which Kirchner makes Halai Aixonides by identifications of some of the names ; but these are quite uncertain, and would suit Melite as well, a deme which serves much better on other grounds. We have no other certain figures of Kekropis for comparison. It is by no means certain that the 17 names belong to Kekropis ; but as they cannot be Acharneis (Oineis), no other deme than Melite, from another phyle, suits. For Hippothontis is also excluded ; otherwise the deme might be Peiraieis, if the big group of names in Hippothontis preserved on this stone be Eleusinioi (see below, p. 63, n. 3).

No. 1740 (Pandionis) is dated by Kirchner before 388 because of Aristophanes Kydathenaieus, " who must be the poet." But there may well have been another man of the name. The restoration of *demotica* and even of the places where they should come on the stone, seems uncertain (this stone too is lost) ; but accepting most of them as they appear in *I.G.*, Kytherrioi is missing. There is room for it below Probalisioi, making 4 Probalisioi (against 5 on No. 1731, a complete

350 B.C., 2 in 341–0 and in 336–5 ; Ikarieis, 4 in 350, 5 in
341–0 ; Phegaieis, 4 in 350, 3 in 341–0. In Oineis : Lakiadai
2 in 360–59, 3 c. 350 ; Tyrmeidai 0 and 1 (perhaps, as Sundwall suggests, alternating with Hippotomadai, another very
small deme, which had one member in 360–59). In Hippothontis : Anakaieis 4 in c. 370–60, 3 in 336–5. In Antiochis :
Eitiaioi 2 in 336–5, 1 in 334–3 ; Palleneis 6 in 336–5, 7 in
334–3. These, and the changes in Pandionis mentioned in
the note below, are the only ones we are sure of ; and
the only changes involving more than one bouleutes are those
in Oaieis, Myrrhinousioi, and Kydathenaieis, which were perhaps due to reorganisation by Demetrius.

It should be clear from this that we cannot even guess, if
we are sensible men, at relative changes in the size of demes ;
still less can we say, with Sundwall, that because there 12

list), one Kytherrios (against 2), 12 Kydathenaieis (against 11), and 7
Myrrhinousioi (against 6).

No. 1753 (also Pandionis) gives most variations of all these lists
(though again there is doubt, as the stone is lost and incomplete) : 5
Myrrhinousioi, 2 Prasieis (3 on No. 1751), 4 Probalisioi (against 5),
10 Paianieis (12 on 1751, and 11 *plus* 1 from Paianieis καθύπερθεν on
1740), 2 Oaieis (against 4). Twenty bouleutai are missing (not 19, as
Kirchner says) ; 2 of these might be one more each to Prasieis and Probalisioi, the remaining 18 to be divided between Paianieis καθύπ.
(perhaps 2), Kydathenaieis (14, 13 ?), and Kytherrioi (2, 3 ?). The
inscription belongs to the end of the fourth century, but before 307 ;
there may have been some redistribution of seats in the boule by
Demetrius of Phaleron.

Some of the third century inscriptions are useful for comparison,
e.g. 678 (Aigeis), 848 (Leontis), 913 (Erechtheis). No. 918 (Leontis, ii.
cent. *init.*) is strange : it corresponds closely enough in general with
848 (209/8 B.C.), except that Sounieis has been transferred to Attalis,
but Skambonidai has only one bouleutes (against 4 in 209, and 3 in
fourth cent.), Phrearrioi only 3 (against 5 or 7 in 209, and 9 in fourth
cent.), and Paionidai, with 3 members in 209 and in the fourth century,
has 10. The coast-trittys is left with only four members. One suspects
a mistake of the stonecutter, confusing Phrearrioi and Paionidai.

(There is one curious fragment of a list, ii² 2366. No title, and the
stone is complete at the top (broken below) ; but it had been clamped
to another stone above it. By demes ; no patronymics. Three cols.
preserved in part, thus :

Kephisieis	[Anagyrasi]oi	Akamantidos
9 names	12	Euxitheos
Euonymeis	Phegousioi	
8	1	

The first two cols. apparently belong to Erechtheis ; Euxitheos is not
given a deme. The stone was found at Eleusis, and is dated fourth
century *init.* Is it a list of men settled in Eleusis after 403/2 ? followed
by a decree defining their privileges, or by an oath taken by them ?
Actually, [Anagyrasi]oi does not fit ; the inscription is written στοι-
χηδόν, and this should be a word of 9 letters. If so, it could not be
from Erechtheis. Similarly, col. i, l. 9 . . . ⁷ . . . . ΗΣ might be a *demoticum* but not from Erechtheis.)

Kydathenaieis (town-trittys, Pandionis) in the boule c. 390
B.C., and 11 c. 340, and 6 from Oa (town-trittys, Oineis) in
360–59 and perhaps 5 in c. 350 (see on No. 1746, p. 51, n. 2),
" ist ' ein Rückgang der ursprünglichen Bevölkerung der
Stadtdemen unzweideutig festgestellt."[1]   Apart from the
fact that some of the evidence is doubtful (see above), and the
distribution of many demes among the town, coast and inland
trittyes uncertain, there is nothing like enough evidence for
a generalization. It is an abuse of statistics. In Pandionis,
in fact, Kydathenaieis probably had its representation increased before the end of the century, and Oaieis (an inland
deme) and Myrrhinous (a coast deme) had theirs decreased ;
and of the other changes enumerated above, of the decreases
two were in town demes, three were in coast demes and two in
probably inland demes ; and of the increases three were in
town demes,[2] one on the coast and three inland.

M. G. Mathieu is so cautious that he will not allow even
approximate conclusions as to the hoplite population of Athens
to be drawn from the epheboi inscriptions (because the phylae
were not certainly equal after Cleisthenes) ; but he thinks it
possible to estimate changes of population within Leontis by
a comparison of the bouleutai in the first half of the fourth
century (I.G. ii² 1742) with the diaitetai and the epheboi in
325–3.[3]   He finds that four demes had a larger percentage of
the 50 bouleutai of the phylê than of the 63 epheboi, that one
had about the same, and four had a smaller percentage :
and argues a decline in population between c. 370 and 325 in
the first class, and an increase in the second. He also, from
a comparison of the epheboi and diaitetai of 325–3, argues that
the population was at that time declining in those demes in
which the epheboi were not twice[4] as many as the diaitetai,
and increasing in those in which they were more than twice as
many (forgetting that there are not so many persons living at

---

[1] Epigr. Beitr., p. 55.

[2] Including Kytherrioi as a town-deme, with Kydathenaieis in
Pandionis, as I think probable, in spite of the fact that Kytheros is
mentioned by Philochorus (ap. Strabo, ix 397) as one of the 12 towns
of Cecrops, before the synoecism, and that it was largely rural in character (Dem. xlii 5).   If I am right, then probably Kydathenaieis and
Kytherrioi had 13 bouleutai between them, divided 12 and 1 or 11
and 2 (see p. 51, n. 2), as Palleneis and Eiteaioi in Antiochis had 8,
divided 7 and 1, or 6 and 2.   (If the fragment 2413 is from a bouleutai-
list—towards the end of the fourth century—we have 12 Kydathenaieis
and 2 Kytherrioi, as well as . . .]ιεῖς with one name, which should be
Paianieis καθύπ.)

[3] Rev. Phil. iii 179 ff. He assumes a redistribution of bouleutai
in 403, and no subsequent change before Demetrius.

[4] He supposes the 63 Leontis epheboi to belong to two years ;
see below, p. 67 ff.

60 as at 18 or 19). These last include Sounion and Phrearrioi
so he supposes an increase in industrial activity in the mines.
This is quite impossible. First, the basis of comparison is not
the same : the bouleutai represented the whole citizen population of the demes, the epheboi and diaitetai were, in all
probability, drawn from the hoplite and higher classes only.
Second, for the industrial activity, the argument ignores the
fact that deme-membership was hereditary, not by residence ;
an increase in mining activity might mean an increase of resi-
dents in the Laurion district, but not of members of the demes.[1]
Thirdly, if we must be careful about the use of figures for whole
phylae, we must avoid altogether using, in this way, figures
for such small units as the epheboi and the diaitetai of single
demes for one year only. If we had figures for a series of years
it would be possible, though it would still apply only to the
richer classes. Especially is this the case with the diaitetai,
very few in number, who, as M. Mathieu himself admits, did
not include half the men of hoplite-census in their 60th year,
for there were many dispensations.[2] From one year to
another in single demes, the epheboi and diaitetai might vary
greatly. Note for example that Thorikos, a considerable
deme, had only one ephebos in 305/4 ; Eleusis, a large one,
and Kydathenaieis no diaitetes in 325/4. We cannot even
argue from the diaitetai of whole phylae ; for in this year,
325–4, there were only three from Pandionis out of 103 (only
two demes out of 10 being represented), and 16 from Kekropis.[3]
Are we to assume that the hoplite population of the former
was but one-fifth, or anything like one-fifth, of the latter ?

We have indeed two definite statements of deme-population,
one for Acharnae in 430, one for Halimous shortly before the
middle of the fourth century. But the 3000 hoplites of
Acharnae (Thuc. ii 20. 4) cannot be accepted. This would
mean more than one-tenth of the hoplite population of Athens,
at least as much as the phyle, Oineis, could provide (Acharnae
had 22 members in the boule, and so, large as it was, should
have had less than half the population of the phyle). In the
case of Halimous, according to Dem. lvii 9—15, there were
not more than 85—90 demotai (of whom 73, we are told, a

<hr>

[1]. Compare p. 46, above, for the demes of mineowners. The comparatively large size of the demes in the Laurion District only proves the
activity in the mines at the end of the sixth century, due to Peisistratus,
and that this activity was mainly one of citizens, or at least of men
given citizenship in 507 ; and that, if there was a redistribution of seats
after 403, they had remained large, as we should anyhow suppose would
be the case.

[2] See the table on p. 29, above, for the approximate number who
would reach their sixtieth year annually c. 325 B.C.

[3] See the tables at the end of this note.

very large proportion, were present at the διαψήφισις, which was held in Athens). The deme had three representatives in the Boule. If this were in right proportion to the population of the phyle, then Leontis had no more than some 1500 members. This is against all our other evidence ; and we must assume either understatement by Demosthenes' client, or that Halimous was much over-represented. Both are possible enough, the latter particularly, because it was a small deme, which might suffer permanently after a catastrophe. Its representation was reduced to two in the third century, and it had no ephebos in 327–6 out of 63 for the phyle—which may be significant. Similarly Leukonoeis and Oion in the same phyle, as already suggested, seem to have been under-represented. But it shows how complex this problem is, and how careful one must be in deduction.

From the numbers of members of the demes as recorded in *Prosopographia Attica* not much can be obtained that is useful. We have large numbers from the demes with most bouleutai,[1] and small numbers from those with only one or two ; but again we get disturbing variations, as we should expect, in the smaller demes. For example, within Aigeis : Ankyleis 2 bouleutai and 98 names recorded, Halai 5 and 195, Diomeeis 1 and 37, Erchieis 6 and 202, Myrrhinoutte 1 and 47, Philaidai 3 and 91 ; but Ikarieis 5 and 128, Ionidai 2 and 30, Teithrasioi 4 and 55.

The following tables give the phylae and demes, with their bouleutai, epheboi and diaitetai as far as known.[2] The bouleutai are given according to the complete lists, where these exist ; where there are variations (before 307 B.C.), the variant figures are given in brackets, to the left of the other figure if of earlier date, to the right if later. Figures for the period of the 12 phylae (after 307) are added in italics, where we have complete lists.

Where totals are given, it means that the list is complete ; where none is given that we have only a fragment. For the epheboi and diaitetai inscriptions, see Note B, below. After

---

[1] There is one apparent exception, Euonymeis : 2 bouleutai and a large deme. But the figure 2, accepted by Sundwall without misgiving, is based only on the incomplete *I.G.* i² 398 (above, p. 51) ; there were 12 bouleutai c. 200 B.C. (ii² 913), and there is no reason to suppose a smaller number in the fifth and fourth centuries. There were 11 epheboi in 305/4, and 4 diaitetai in 325/4. Probably Anagyrasioi is another such case : on i² 398 space for four names (but nothing inscribed) ; in 200 B.C. 8 bouleutai.

[2] One or two of the figures are restored, but with practical certainty, in *I.G.* These I give without further comment.

the name of each deme I have added in brackets the number of known *demotai*, as shown in *Prosopographia Attica*.[1]

[1] With some adjustments, for Kirchner's enumeration is not always systematic; for example, among Anagyrasioi: " Λ . . . cf. Φιλόνοθος Λ . . ." where Λ . . . is counted ; but " Φιλωνίδης Δ . . ." where Δ . . . is not counted. I have included all incomplete names ; and as well some omissions that I have noted—e.g. Anaximenes and Nikostratos of Halimous (Dem. lvii 59), who should certainly be in, whether we believe the truth of the story told about them or not. Women whose husbands' demes are known but not their fathers', are excluded. In the case of two or more demes of the same name in different phylae, I have distributed the whole number between the phylae in the same proportion as the known numbers : e.g. Halai Araphenides in Aigeis 55 known, Halai Aixonides in Kekropis 34 ; 314 names in all are known ; therefore I give 195 to Aigeis, 119 to Kekropis.

I. ERECHTHEIS.

	Bouleutai.			Epheboi.	Diaitetai.	
	408/7 (i[2] 398)	336/5 (ii[2] 1700)	c. 200 (ii[2] 913)	305/4 (ii[2] 478)	330/29 (ii[2] 1924)	325/4 (ii[2] 1926)
(a) Agryleis (83) { καθύπ. 2 / ὑπέν. 1 }			3[3]	1[3]		0
(a) Euonymeis (227)	?[1]		12	11	1(+?)	4
(a) Themakeis (25)		1	—[2]	1		0
(b) Anagyrasioi (142)	?[1]		8	5		1
(b) Kedoi (44)	2		2	?		1
(b) Lamptreis (391) { καθύπ. 2(+?) / ὑπέν. }			10[3]	?[3]		3
(b?) Pambotadai (34)			2	1?		0
(c) Kephisieis (250)	?[1]		8	6(+?)	1(+?)	2
(c) Pergaseis (71) { καθύπ. 2 / ὑπέν. 2 }			3[3]	1?[3]		0
(c?) Phegousioi (23)		1	1	1?		2
(c?) Sybridai (22)			1	0?		0
Totals			50			13
(a) Town-demes (335)			15	13		4
(b) Coast-demes (611)			22	6+		5
(c) Inland-demes (366)			13	8+		4

[1] For the figures in this inscription, see above, p. 55, n. 1.

[2] Themakeis in Ptolemais after c. 224/3.

[3] Part of Agryleis, of Lamptreis and of Pergaseis in Antigonis 307—200 B.C.

II. AIGEIS.

	Bouleutai. c. 350, 341/0, 336/5 (ii² 1747, 1749, 1700)	276/5 (ii² 678)	Epheboi. 305/4 (ii² 478)	Diaitetai. 330/29 (ii² 1924)	325/4 (1926)
(a) Ankyleis (98)	2	7[2]			0
(a) Bateis (45)	(2) 1	—[2]			0
(a) Diomeeis (37)	1	—[2]			1
(a) Hestiaieis (22)	1	1			1
(a) Kollyteis (106)	3	4		2 (+?)	2
(a) Koloneis (58)	2	2			0
(b) Araphenioi (47)	2	2			0
(b) Halai Araphenides (195)	5	8		1 (+?)	2
(b) Phegaieis (68)	(4) 3	3	1		0
(b) Philaidai (91)	3	3			0
(b?) Erikeeis (23)	1	2			0
(b?) Myrrhinoutte (47)	1	3			0
(b?) Otryneis (60)	1	3			0
(c) Erchieis (202)	6	10			2
(c) Gargettioi (138)	4	—[2]	(2 in Antigonis)		1
(c) Ikarieis (128)	(4)[1] 5	—[2]			2
(c) Kydantidai (44)	(1) 2	1			2
(c) Plotheis (46)	1	2			1
(c) Teithrasioi (55)	4	4			0
(c?) Ionidai (30)	2	1	4 (?)		0
Totals	50	50			14
(a) Town-demes (366)	10	8			4
(b) Coast-demes (531)	16	24			2
(c) Inland (643)	24	18			8

[1] No. 1747 can be restored with reasonable certainty. There are three columns; the top of the stone is broken off and lost. 19 bouleutai and 8 demes are missing: i.e. 27 lines, 9 to the col. So all the demes were represented; five of the missing demes had one each (as on 1749, the complete list of 341/0), and one of the three bigger missing demes (Erchieis, Teithrasioi, and Ikarieis) had one bouleutes fewer than on 1749 (Phegaieis had one more). So restore thus:

Erchieis	Teithrasioi	Ikarieis
6 names	4 names	4 names
Diomeeis	Erikeeis	Myrrhinoutte
1 name	1 name	1 name
	Hestiaieis	Otryneis
	1 name	1 name

To make the missing part fit, with 9 more lines to each column, the three bigger demes must each have had an even number of bouleutai; so Ikarieis is the deme with one fewer.

[2] Part of Ankyleis, and Bateis, Gargettioi, Diomeeis and Ikarieis in Antigonis or Demetrias 307—200. Shortly before 200 Gargettioi had only 2 bouleutai (ii² 912).

III. PANDIONIS.

	Bouleutai. c. 390? c. 340, c. 310 (ii² 1740 ; 1751 & 1753)²	Epheboi.	Diaitetai. 330/29 (ii² 1924)	329/8 (ii² 1925)	325/4 (ii² 1926)
(a) Kydathenaieis (295)	12 (11, 13?)				o
(a?) Kytherrioi (63)¹	1? (2, 3?)				o
(b) Angeleis (61)	3				o
(b) Myrrhinousioi (136)	7 (6, 5)				o
(b) Prasieis (35)	3				o
(b) Probalisioi (91)	4? (5)			1 (+?)	1
(b) Steirieis (74)	3				o
(c) Konthylidai (24)	1				o
(c) Oaieis (67)	4 (2)				o
(c) Paianieis (377) {καθύπ. 1 / ὑπέν. 11 }			2 (+?)		2
Totals	50	—	—	—	3
(a) Town-demes (358)	13				o
(b) Coast-demes (397)	20				1
(c) Inland-demes (468)	17				2

¹ See above, p. 53, n. 2, for the trittys of Kytherrioi.
² See p. 51, n. 2, for the date of 1740, and for 1753.

IV. LEONTIS.

	Bouleutai. c. 365—335 (ii² 1742 ; 1700, 1752)	c. 199 (ii² 918 ; (cp. 848)	Epheboi. c. 326/5 (Eph. Arch. 1918)	Diaitetai. 330/29 (ii³ 1924)	329/8 (1925)	325/4 (1926)
(a) Cholleidai (110)	2	7	4			4
(a) Halimousioi (79)	3	2	0			0
(a) Leukonoeis (153)	3	5	5			1
(a) Skambonidai (79)	3	1	2		2(+?)	1
(a?) Kettioi (55)	3	2	6			0
(a?) Potamioi (51) { καθύπ.	2 }	?²	1			0
ὑπέν.	1 }	?	2			
(b) Deiradiotai (55)	2	1	1			3
(b) Phrearrioi (191)	9	3	13	1 (+?)	1(+?)	2
(b) Potamioi Deir. (35)	2	?²	5			0
(b) Sounieis (154)	4	—¹	10			1
(c) Aithalidai (94)	2	5	1			0
(c) Eupyridai (97)	2	3	1			0
(c) Hekaleieis (28)	1	—¹	1		1(+?)	0
(c) Paionidai (59)	3	10	0		1(+?)	0
(c?) Hybadai (36)	2	1	5			0
(c?) Koloneis (23)	2	?²	2			0
(c?) Kropidai (39)	1	2	0			0
(c?) Oion (140)	1	4	2			0
(c?) Pelekes (24)	2	2	2			0
Totals	50	²	63			12
(a) Town-demes (527)	17	18 ?	20			6
(b) Coast-demes (435)	17	4	29			6
(c) Inland (540)	16	28 ?	14			0

(The trittyes are uncertain, this distribution depending on Löper's view that in No. 1742 the demes are given in the order of trittyes ; which is anything but proved, the separation of the Potamioi demes being definitely against it. The location of the inland trittys in Attica is also unknown, and it has been omitted on the map at the end of the volume.)

¹ Hekaleieis in Ptolemais, Sounieis in Attalis after 200 B.C.

² Two lines on the inscr. erased after the 7 Cholleidai, and two names wanting to make 50. See also p. 51, n. 2, above.

V. AKAMANTIS.

	Bouleutai. 378/7 and 336/5 (ii² 1741, 1700)	Epheboi. 305/4 (ii² 478)	Diaitetai. 329/8 (ii² 1925)	325/4 (ii² 1926)
(a) Kerameis (151)		3	1(+?)	0
(a?) Cholargeis (123)		2		1
(a?) Eiresidai (21)	1	1 ?		0
(a?) Hermeioi (54)	2			0
(a?) Iphistiadai (40)				0
(a?) Porioi (38)				1
(b) Kephale (130)		5		0
(b) Thorikioi (134)		1	1(+?)	2
(b?) Kikynneis (40)		2		0
(c?) Eiteaioi (32)				0
(c?) Hagnousioi (99)	4 (+?)		1?[1]	1
(c?) Prospaltioi (90)	5		1 (+?)	4
(c?) Sphettioi (178)			1 (+?)	0
Total	—	—	—	9
(a) Town-demes (427?)[2]				2?
(b) Coast-demes (367?)				2?
(c) Inland-demes (336?)				5?

[1] Another name is preserved without the *demoticum*; identified by Kirchner, but very uncertainly, with an Hagnousios.

[2] The distribution among trittyes is uncertain. Since the publication of *I.G.* i² 900, it has been generally accepted that Cholargeis, and with it all the other demes previously given to the town-trittys except Kerameis, formed the inland-trittys (for the town-trittys was Κεραμέων, and on that stone we have mention of Χολαργέων τριττύς) : see Hiller *ad loc.*, and Solders, *Die ausserstädt. Kulte.* But this involves not only making the town-trittys very small, but putting Sphettos (not far from Koropi, in the heart of the Mesogeia) into the coast-trittys, and with it Hagnous and Prospalta, and greatly overweighting it—(a) 151 names ; (b) 734 ; (c) 286. I find this very inconvincing. See also p. 49, n. 2, above.

ii² 2411 may be from a bouleutai-list ; if it is, then 8 (+?) to Kephale, 7 Sphettioi, 6 Cholargeis. From which we may reasonably guess at the following list :—

Kerameis	6 or 7	Porioi	1		Eiteaioi	1
Cholargeis	6	Kephale	8		Hagnousioi	4
Eiresidai	1	Thorikioi	6 or 5		Prospaltioi	5
Hermeioi	2	Kikynneis	2		Sphettioi	7
Iphistiadai	1					

(a) Town-demes : 17 or 7.
(b) Coast : 16 or 32.
(c) Inland : 17 or 11.

VI. OINEIS.

	Bouleutai. c. 370, 360/59, c. 350 336/5 (ii² 1745 ; 1698, 1746, 1700)	Diaitetai. 325/4 (ii² 1926)
(a) Boutadai (36)	1	0
(a) Hippotomadai (12)	1 (0?)	0
(a) Lakiadai (97)	2 (3)	0
(a) Oa (105)	6	2
(a) Perithoidai (69)	3	0
(a) Tyrmeidai (18)	0 (1)	0
(a?) Epikephisioi (42)	2	0
(a?) Lousieis (30)	1	0
(a?) Pteleasioi (23)	1	1
(b) Kothokidai (57)	2	0
(b) Phylasioi (83)	(3) 2	0
(b) Thriasioi (101)	7	0
(c) Acharneis (452)	22	8
Totals	50	11
(a) Town-demes (432)	17	3
(b) Coast-demes (241)	11	0
(c) Inland-deme (452)	22	8

VII. KEKROPIS.

	Bouleutai. c. 370, 336/5 (ii² 1698, 1743, 1700)	Epheboi. 334/3 (ii² 1156)	Diaitetai. 325/4 (ii² 1926)
(a) Meliteis (257)	17 (+?)?²	11(+?)?²	3
(a) Xypetaiones (108)		2	4
(b) Aixoneis (237)		7	2
(b) Halai Aixonides (119)	4 (+?)		3
(c) Athmoneis (141)			2
(c) Daidalidai (17)	1	1	1
(c) Phlyeis (224)¹	2 (+?)		1
(c) Pitheis (82)	3	2	0
(c) Sypalettioi (83)	2		0
(c) Trinemeeis (29)			0
(?) Epieikidai (17)			0
(?) Kikynneis (19)			0
Total	—	—	16
(a) Town demes (365)			7
(b) Coast-demes (356)			5
(c) Inland-demes (576)			4

¹ Solders, p. 4, following Svoronos, places Phlya S. of Chalandri and extending as far as Kaisariane E. of Athens, and includes it in the town-trittys.

² For ii² 1698 see above, p. 51, n. 2 ; and for the epheboi, below, p. 67. If ii² 2377 is part of a bouleutai-list (of Kekropis and Hippothontis), then we have [Μελιτ]ῆς followed by eight names with gaps between them, covering 14 lines ; and so 14 (+?) bouleutai. See next list.

If ii² 2383 were from a bouleutai-list, it would be very interesting. Parts of two cols., 11 names of one deme (Aixoneis or Phlya, if bouleutai) on one, 15 (+?) of another, certainly Melite, on the other. Of these 15 four are apparently closely related : Philonides s. of Onetor, Philon s. of Onetor, Onetor s. of Proxenos, and Aischetades s. of Proxenos. Were they all members of the boule in the same year ?

(No. 1156, the epheboi inscription, shows the dangers of rash identification : there are five names of an unknown deme, none of which—except perhaps Chairion—Chairionides Phlyeus—is found in any Kekropid deme ; and one of them, Antiphanes s. of Antiphates, is found twice (and only twice) elsewhere, in one family, but Kytherrioi in Pandionis.)

VIII. HIPPOTHONTIS.

	Bouleutai. c. 370, 336/5 (ii² 1698, 1700)	Epheboi. 305/4 (ii² 478)	Diaitetai. 325/4 (ii² 1926)
(a) Keiriadai (39)	3		0
(a) Koileis (78)			0
(a) Korydalloi (14)			0
(a) Peiraieis (235)	?³		2
(a) Thymaitadai (26)			0
(a?) Eroiadai (21)	?²		0
(b) Eleusinioi (198)	?³		0
(b) Kopreioi (41)	3		1
(b) Oinaioi (72)	?¹		2
(b?) Anakaieis (39)	4 (3)	1	0
(b?) Elaiousioi (30)	1²	1	0
(c) Dekeleeis (64)	?¹		0
(c?) Oion (18)			2
(?) Acherdousioi (43)			1
(?) Auridai (24)			0
(?) Azenieis (71)	3		1
(?) Hamaxanteieis (64)			0
	—	—	—
Total			9
			—
(a) Town-demes (413)			2
(b) Coast-demes (380)			3
(c) Inland-demes (82 + ?)			2+?

¹ Six names of one deme : Dekeleeis restored by Kirchner on the strength of one quite uncertain identification. Oinaioi would suit as well. See below.

² E[laíousioi], suppl. Kirchner. Eroiadai is also possible.

³ On 1698 there is a group of 11 names, of which the first is L¡ .... This might be the *demoticum* Eleusinioi, in which case ten bouleutai from Eleusis ; if not, then 11 (+?) from either Eleusis or Peiraeus (the latter acc. to Kirchner and Sundwall).

If ii² 2377 is from a bouleutai-list, then c. 360 Azenieis had 2 bouleutai (3 on 1698), Hamaxanteieis 2, Anakaieis 3 (4 on 1698, 3 on 1700), Dekeleeis 4 (see above), Elaiousioi 1 (see above).

A most unsatisfactory phyle. The trittys-distribution of many demes is also quite uncertain.

IX. AIANTIS.

	Diaitetai. 325/4 (ii² 1926)
(a) Phalereis (168)	1
(b) Marathonioi (247)	1
(b) Oinaioi (36)	1
(b) Rhamnousioi (203)	4
(b) Trikorysioi (96)	1
(c) Aphidnaioi (229)	1
Total	9
(1) Town-deme (168)	1
(b) Coast-demes (582)	7
(c) Inland-deme (229)	1

No certain figures of bouleutai for any deme. On ii 1700 are 4 names, all of one unknown deme. If ii² 2400 (c. 340 B.C.) is part of a bouleutai-list, then 6 from Marathon and 5 or 6 from Rhamnus ; which do not seem enough. If ii² 2423 (c. 300) is one (our only point of comparison is Anaphlystioi in Antiochis with 10 names, the same number as on the complete list of 334/3), there were 7 (+?) bouleutai of an unknown deme, and 9 (+?) Phalereis ; this would suit well enough.

X. ANTIOCHIS.

	Bouleutai. 336/5, 334/3 (ii² 1700, 1750)	Diaitetai. 325/4 (ii² 1926)
(a) Alopekeis (255)	10	1
(a?) Koloneis (23)	2	0
(a?) Krioeis (47)	1	0
(b) Aigilieis (93)	6	2
(b) Amphitropaieis (73)	2	0
(b) Anaphlystioi (172)	10	0
(b) Ateneis (47)	3	0
(b) Besaieis (28)	2	0
(b) Semachidai (37)	1	1
(b) Thoraieis (55)	4	0
(c) Eroiadai (21)	1	1
(c) Palleneis (187)	(6) 7	2
(c?) Eiteaioi (20)	(2) 1	0
Totals	50	7
(a) Town-demes (325)	13	1
(b) Coast-demes (505)	28	3
(c) Inland-demes (228)	9	3

Löper, followed by Kirchner, puts Kolonos, Krioa and Semachidai among the inland-demes, on the assumption that the arrangement of demes on 1750, the complete list, is by trittyes ; but even so the order is disturbed (Krioeis following Alopeke), and there is some evidence for placing Semachidai in the mining district and so in the coast-trittys. Still the distribution of strength is remarkably one-sided.

E

Taking those demes only the number of whose bouleutai is certain or probable, with the trittyes as given above (many of which are admittedly doubtful), we have, for six phylae :

	No. of names in P.A.	Bouleutai.	
(a) Town-demes	2343	85 (1 in 27.5)	
(b) Coast-demes	2720	114 (1 in 23.9)	out of 300.
(c) Inland-demes	2697	101 (1 in 26.1)	

Of the remaining four phylae, in Akamantis none of the three districts is specially prominent (unless Sphettos and other demes are put in the coast trittys, see above, p. 60, n. 2) ; in Kekropis, the city-trittys with Melite and Xypetaiones, is predominant ; in Hippothontis, the city again, with Peiraeus and others ; in Aiantis the coast. The numbers of the bouleutai for each district shows that in the time of Cleisthenes the paralia (including, it will be remembered, the mining area and all Attica west of Mt. Aigaleos) was the most populous, the city-district the least, though probably little less populous than the mesogeia. If the proportion of bouleutai to the number of names preserved in *Prosopographia Attica* is significant, there will have been some decline in the coast-demes after Cleisthenes ; or else, as many of these demes were farthest from Athens, fewer came into town to hold office or conduct business, in such a way that their names would be preserved.

It is obvious from the figures that we cannot draw any conclusions about the population of the individual demes from numbers of epheboi and diaitetai, especially the latter. Note for example in Hippothontis, 2 diaitetai each from Peiraeus, Oinoe and Oion, and none from Eleusis ; one each from Alopeke, Eroiadai and Semachidai in Antiochis, none from Anaphlystioi. We have nothing like enough evidence. But a few more lists, and how illuminating they might be. It may be that Thorikos had only 1 ephebos in 305–4 and Kephale 5, because the former, near the mines, was poor, the latter with its vineyards well-to-do ; it may be that the Teithrasioi, with 4 bouleutai, but no diaitetes and only 55 known members, were mainly hillmen, too poor and too obscure to hold office.[1] We should know a lot more about Athens if we could establish facts such as these. We cannot as yet even guess ; but with more evidence we may be able to.

---

[1] For the site of Teithrasioi, see Möbius, *Ath. Mitt.* xlix, pp. 1—3.

NOTE B

THE EPHEBOI AND DIAITETAI INSCRIPTIONS

THERE are only three epheboi inscriptions which help us to estimate the total hoplite population of Athens : *I.G.* ii² 1156, the epheboi of Kekropis in 334-3, *Eph. Arch.* 1918, p. 73ff, those of Leontis c. 327-6, and *I.G.* ii² 478, which gives some figures for seven phylae (out of 12) in 305-4, but only those of Erechtheis are sufficiently complete for our purpose.[1]

(1) No. 1156 is in two columns, the upper parts of which are missing. In col. 2 are 22 names, 11 of an unknown deme, Aixoneis 7, Xypetaiones 2, Pitheis 2. In col. 1, Daidalidai with one name is at the bottom, above that 5 names of an unknown deme, and 2 of another. The 11 (+ ?) are probably Meliteis, the 5 Athmoneis, Halaieis, or Phlyeis. This leaves two of these three larger demes, Sypalettos, and three very small demes to be supplied. So probably 43—45 names in all.

(2) The 63 epheboi of Leontis are generally supposed to be the recruits of two years, 325-4 and 324-3. This in itself is very unlikely. The two classes of epheboi did not form one body ; the first year served in Peiraeus, the second in the forts, from Eleusis to Rhamnus. They had different commanders, the first the two strategoi ἐπὶ τῷ Πειραιεῖ and ἐπὶ τῇ Ἀκτῇ (or τῇ Μουνυχίᾳ), the second the strategos ἐπὶ τῇ χώρᾳ; different sophronistai and didaskaloi, and a different kosmetes. These 63 epheboi crown all three generals, Leosthenes (general ἐπὶ τῇ χώρᾳ), Dikaiogenes (in Peiraeus) and Pherekleides (in Akte), their kosmetes, Philokles Φορμίωνος Ἐροιάδης, and their didaskalos, epimeletes, and sophronistes. But if they are epheboi of two years, half of them had had nothing to do with Leosthenes, to the other half Dikaiogenes and Pherekleides were nothing ; only half had been cared for by Philokles :

[1] Some of the figures for other demes (see the tables given above) are interesting in themselves : especially would be 4 epheboi from Ionidai (Aigeis), apparently a very small deme, but neither the name of the deme nor the number of the ephebes is quite certain ; as so often, the restoration in the new edition of *I.G.* gives a misleading air of certainty—see Elter, p. 55-6. (The ten Erchieis, accepted by Beloch, are very doubtful ; it is not even certain that they belong all to one deme.) But we want figures for the phylae to help us for the whole population. Beloch takes all the figures we have, 23 demes with 73 names (we actually have 25 demes with 82 names : he omits Ionidai and an unknown deme of Oineis with 5 epheboi), and says : "nach diesem Verhältniss würden alle 140 Demen 445 Epheben gestellt haben." This is to ignore the varying sizes of demes, and is quite unreliable.

the kosmetes of the other year, with the sophronistes and the didaskalos, remains unhonoured. The inscription recording the honour was set up in Rhamnus, where the epheboi of the first year had not yet served. Is it likely? Is it not more probable that they are epheboi of one year, honouring at the end of their two years of service their generals of each year, their kosmetes, who was with them in their first year, and the didaskalos, who had probably been with them all the time?

Why then have all—Leonardos the editor, Beloch, Mathieu, Colin—supposed that we have epheboi of two years? Because Philokles the well-known general in Munichia in 325-4 (when he admitted Harpalus) was kosmetes of the epheboi in 324-3, and was deprived of his office and tried for his part in the Harpalus affair (Dein. iii 15) ; and therefore identical with the Philokles of this inscription. That being so, Pherekleides cannot have been strategos in Munichia in 325-4 ; therefore he was strategos in 324-3, when Philokles was kosmetes. Leosthenes again was not strategos ἐπὶ τῇ χώρᾳ in 323-2, when he commanded the forces abroad, and was killed ; he therefore held this office in 324-3, and we have the three generals of *one* year 324-3, of whom one commanded the second-year epheboi, the others the first-year epheboi. Therefore we have epheboi of two years.

There is, however, no evidence that Philokles the general was kosmetes in 324-3. His deme and patronymic are unknown. What Deinarchus says, after some mention of the harbours and docks in Philokles' charge, is : ὁ μὲν δῆμος ἅπας οὔτ' ἀσφαλὲς οὔτε δίκαιον νομίζων εἶναι παρακαταθέσθαι τοὺς ἑαυτοῦ παῖδας ἀπεχειροτόνησεν αὐτὸν ἀπὸ τῆς τῶν ἐφήβων ἐπιμελείας. Till the discovery of our inscription this was thought to mean his office of general in Munichia, which did in fact involve the care of the first-year epheboi.[1] That is right. Philokles was dismissed from his strategia, before July 324 therefore, when first the outcry over the scandal arose ; and Colin's dates must be modified. Philokles was a very common name at Athens ; there are 51 instances of it in *Prosopographia Attica* (including one Eroiades, trierarch in 323-2, who may well be our kosmetes ; another was archon in 322-1). This avoids as well the necessity of supposing, as Mathieu must, that Philokles was acquitted at his trial in Jan. 323, and restored to his office of kosmetes and crowned at the end of the year ; a

---

[1] Ἐπιμελεῖσθαι, is not a technical term used of the kosmetes, as Mathieu implies. If it is necessary to show this, it is used not of the kosmetes, but of the sophronistai in *Const. Ath.* 42. 2—3, the passage to which Mathieu refers ; it is used of the sophronistes of the Kekropid epheboi (*I.G.* ii² 1156), of the epheboi themselves in their duties, of a general, a phylarchos, a taxiarchos (*S.E.G.* iii 115, 116, 122).

supposition not very likely in itself, and contradicted by Dem. *Epist.* iii 31.

With this identification disappears the whole case for thinking the epheboi of this inscription to belong to both years. They were not those enrolled in 325–4, when Philokles, not Pherekleides, was general at Munichia ; nor those of 324–3, for in that case they would have served till July 322, and set up the inscription after that, when Leosthenes was dead.[1] But 326–5 or 327–6 will do.[2]

(3) ii[2] 478. In this inscription (in four columns for the twelve phylae), in Erechtheis we have six names of an unknown deme, but the beginning of the deme is uncertain, for the names are on two fragments which do not join ; then Agryle and one name (half of the deme was in Antigonis), Euonymeis and 11 names, Anagyrasioi and 5, then – – –]s and one name, – – – and one name[3] ; then on another fragment which does not join – – – (a deme) and one name (– – –Ἑστιαίου), – – –]s and one name. (Akamantis then begins.) That is, eight demes out of the eleven in the phyle. Themakeis and Pergaseis (half of it now in Antigonis) fit best the two places – – –]s. (Kirchner restores Themakeis as the deme of the son of Hestiaios ; but this is quite arbitrary.) There were three other small demes, Pambotadai, Sybridai and Phegousioi, any two of which would do for the other vacant spaces with one name each. The third may have had no ephebos (cf. the Leontis list). This leaves Kephisieis (8 bouleutai in 200 B.C.), part of Lamptreis (part was in Antigonis ; the whole had 10 bouleutai in 200), and Kedoi for the 6 names at the beginning. Doubtless therefore at least another 5 or 6 names ; so c. 33 in all (though it was possible for a large deme to have only one or two epheboi, as Thorikos in Akamantis this year).

Of many small and doubtful fragments of lists the following seem most likely to be of epheboi : ii[2] 2388 (Aigeis, c. 350 B.C.[4]), 2370 (Pandionis, c. 370 B.C.), 2382 (Leontis, 360–50), 2410 (Leontis and Akamantis, after 330, as very much restored

[1] Actually the identification of Leosthenes with the general of the Lamian War is not certain ; but we need not doubt it.

[2] Four pairs of epheboi in this inscription, each of the same deme, have the same patronymic, so either twins or second or more distant cousins. (One pair have the same name as well as the same father's name and deme—cf. Dem. *c. Boeotum*—certainly cousins.) These also show the dangers of identification so freely indulged in in *I.G.*, though relationship in such cases is always probable. (So in *I.G.* ii[2] 1926, the diaitetai inscription, there are two pairs with the same name and deme.)

[3] The *editio maior* gives two more lines after this, either two names, or a demo and a name, not given in *I.G.*[2].

[4] For the date of the ephebic institution see above, p. 8, n. 3.

by Koehler[1]), and 2384 (Kekropis, 360—50 B.C.). Tabulated these give the following figures (I add in brackets figures from the certain inscriptions—see the tables, pp. 56 ff., above) :

II	Araphenioi	3	V	Thorikioi	3?(1)
	Gargettioi	4(+?)(2)		Kerameis	7?(3)
	Ikarieis	1		?	3
	Kollyteis	2			
	?	3	VII	Sypalettioi	3(+?)
				?	3
III	Kydathenaieis	8(+?)			
	Oaieis	3(+?)			
	?	6			
IV	Halimousioi	1(+?) (0)			
	Kettioi	3(6)			
	Leukonoeis	5(5)			
	Potamioi	2(1-2)			
	Cholleidai	5(4)			
	?	6			
	?	2			

Diaitetai. *I.G.* ii² 1924, 1925, and 1926 are certainly lists of diaitetai. The first two are fragmentary, and are arranged by phylae, but not by demes as well, though the *demoticum* is added ; so that in no case can we be sure that we have all the diaitetai of a deme. No. 1926 is complete for all the phylae, and the arrangement is by both phylae and demes.

No. 1927 (after 350 B.C.) in all probability is not a list of diaitetai. It is an inscription recorded by Chandler,[2] now lost ; four columns were read by him, one for each of the last 4 phylae ; arranged by demes. It recorded 24 names in Kekropis, 19 in Hippothontis, 24 in Aiantis, 23 in Antiochis (with the possibility of a few more names in each not read by Chandler) ; distributed, as in No. 1926, very unequally among the demes—e.g. Meliteis 2, Xypetaiones (a much smaller deme) 6, Eleusis 3, Dekeleeis 5. There will have been presumably some 230–50 names for all the phylae. This is too many for diaitetai to judge from No. 1926, and is rather too high for the number of men of the hoplite census reaching the age of 60 (above, p. 29) ; but there were three letters remaining from the title : T above the first column, A above the *third*, I above the last ; and since we know only two names of magistrates ending in -ται, διαιτηταί and βουλευταί, and it cannot be the

---

[1] The restoration is repeated in *I.G.*², misleadingly, for Fourmont's transcription, on which it is all, somewhat arbitrarily, based, is not given.

[2] *Inscr. Antiq.* pt. ii, No. 107, p. 70.

latter, Kirchner, though with hesitation, accepts it as one of
the diaitetai-lists. But T.AI (for there is nothing recorded
above col. 2) does not fit διαιτηταί; and, if it did, the title
would still be quite unlike those of Nos. 1924-6. I would
rather suppose a misreading on Chandler's part (Ἀθηναίᾳ
ΤΗΙ ΥΤΙ] E [I] ΑΙ or ΠΟΛ] I [A] ΔΙ ?—a dedication).

No. 2409 (c. 330 B.C.) might be from a list of diaitetai; though
it may be from a casualty-list. Five incomplete columns remain, broken at the top, one phyle per column. Another stone
(with the other five phylae) originally fitted on to the right.
Demes are given, but in any order; no patronymics (so not
epheboi). We have 7+ names each from Erechtheis, Aigeis,
Pandionis, and Leontis, 8+ from Akamantis. The phylae
then were more evenly distributed than on 1926; and many
demes there unrepresented have at least one name.

i² 847 (mid. fifth cent.?) may also be from a list of diaitetai:
remains of two cols., broken top and bottom, patronymics
given, but not *demotica*. On col. i 9 names of an unknown
phyle, on col. ii 9 names of another, followed by Ἀκαμαντίδος
(where the stone is broken). If the usual order was followed,
the 9 names on col. ii will be from Leontis. One of the names
on col. i is . . .]τος Ἑστιαιο; the last word may be a patronymic,
but is more likely, from its position on the stone, Ἑστιαιό(θεν)
(the deme added to distinguish from a namesake), in which
case the 9 of col. i will be from Aigeis, and Pandionis will have
come in between.

Tabulating these two uncertain lists, we have (with the certain
figures from Nos. 1924-6—see above, p. 56 ff.—added in brackets)

Fifth Century I	c. 330 B.C. 7+ (no *demotica* legible)	
II 9+	Halai Araph.	1(1, 2)
	Diomeeis	1(1)
	Ikarieis	1(2)
	Kollyteis	1(2)
	Kydantidai	1(2)
	Myrrhinoutte	1(0)
	Philaidai	1(0)
III	Kydathenaieis	1(0)
	Paianieis	3(2)
	Prasieis?	1(0)
	Probalisioi	1(1)
	Steirieis	1(0)

Fifth Century		
IV 9+	Aithalidai	1(0)
	Deiradiotai	1(3)
	Oion	1(0)
	Skambonidai	1(2, 1)
	Hybadai	1(0)
	Phrearrioi	2(1, 2)
V	Hagnousioi	1(1)
	Iphistiadai	1(0)
	Kerameis	1(1, 0)
	Prospaltioi	1(1, 4)
	Sphettioi	2(1, 0)
	Cholargeis	2(1)

(As the names are not given on No. 2409 in order of demes, any of these demes may have had more diaitetai than are given above.)

Hondius (*S.E.G.* iii 142) has suggested the following inscriptions to be from lists of diaitetai or klerouchoi : *I.G.* ii[2] 1698, 2370, 2372, 2377, 2382, 2384, 2388, 2393, 2410, 2411, 2413, and 2434 ; but of these 1698 and 2413 are in all probability from bouleutai-lists (above, p. 51, n. 2), 2411 probably and 2377 possibly from bouleutai-lists (pp. 60, 62–63), 2410 is known only from the very confused transcription of Fourmont (see above, p. 69–70), and 2434 is mid-third century B.C. (and therefore certainly not a clerouchoi-list), and probably a bouleutai-list.   Taking only, then, Nos. 2370, 2372, 2377, 2382, 2384, 2388, and 2393, and tabulating, we would have :

		Diaitetai.	*Bouleutai.*
II	Halai	8(2)	5
	Araphenioi	3(0)	2
	Gargettioi	4(1)	4
	Ikarieis	6(+), 1 (2)	4—5
	Kollyteis	2(2)	3
	?	4	
	?	4(+?)	
III	Kydathenaieis	8+(0)	11—12
	Oaieis	3(0)	4
	?	6	

		Diaitetai.	Bouleutai.
IV	Kettioi	3(0)	3
	Leukonoeis	5(1)	3
	Skambonidai	1(+?) (2, 1)	3
	Cholleidai	5(4)	2
	?	3(+?)	
VII	Meliteis	13?(3)	17?
	Sypalettioi	2—3(0)	2
VIII	Azenieis	2(1)	3
	Hamaxanteieis	2(0)	?
	Anakaieis	3(0)	3—4
	Dekeleeis	4(0)	?
	Elaiousioi	1(0)	1?
	Eleusinioi	1(0)	?
	Koileis	2(0)	?
	Oinaioi	4(2)	?
	Peiraieis	1(2)	?
	?	2	
IX	Marathon	1+?(1)	?
	Oinaioi	1(1)	?
	Trikorysioi	1(1)	?
	?	2	

(the figures in brackets being those of the certain diaitetai of the tables on pp. 56 ff.).

It can be seen from this that not only are the numbers in nearly every case much higher than those of the certain diaitetai, but that they are equal in the aggregate to the number of bouleutai, where these are known (namely, c. 70 and c. 71). This would suggest about 500 diaitetai, a number equal to that of the epheboi (above, p. 10), that is the men of sixty equally numerous with the boys of eighteen, which is obviously absurd. That is why I consider most of these to be epheboi inscriptions (see above, p. 69-70). In any case, lists which may equally well be diaitetai or clerouchoi are of no value for statistical purposes.

NOTE C

THE SIZE OF ATHENIAN FAMILIES, AND THE EXPOSURE OF CHILDREN[1]

SOME scholars have expressed doubt whether it is correct, for Athens, to multiply the number of males between 18 and 59 by four to get the approximate total population : in view of the well-known smallness of Athenian families, they say, $3\frac{1}{2}$ or even 3 would be the better factor.

Beloch multiplies by four, but on the basis of one modern census only, that of Italy of 1881[2] ; and it is as well to consider the matter more thoroughly. Here are some figures for modern countries (for England and Wales, from the census reports, and from the *Statistical Abstract for the United Kingdom for* 1913 *and* 1917–30 ; for foreign countries, from the *Statistical Abstract for Foreign Countries for* 1901–1912, and the *League of Nations Statistical Year-Book* 1931–2). (See pp. 76 and 77.)

The distribution of age-groups in a population depends on birth-rate, infant death-rate (mortality among children less than a year old), and general death-rate ; also on migration ; but most of all on the variations in the birth and death-rates over a period of time ; a steadily declining birth-rate will result in a relatively larger age-group 20—59, and increasing birth-rate a relatively larger age-group 0—19. The increasing longevity in modern European countries is reflected in a general increase in the relative size of the age-group 60+ ; the decreasing birth-rate in a general relative decrease of that of the age-group 0—19 and consequent relative increase of the group 20—59. Migration affects men more than women, and men of the age-group 20—39 more than of other groups ; countries with a large immigration will have relatively more men in this group, countries from which there is much emigration relatively fewer. The selection of statistics for this table has been made to illustrate this, and to include : (1) most Mediterranean countries ; (2) countries with a high birth-rate and high death-rate (as Bulgaria and Portugal), with low birth-rate and low death-rate (as England and Denmark), and those

[1] In getting material for this note from statistical tables of modern countries, I have received much help from Mr. T. H. Marshall of the London School of Economics, and Mr. J. Cunnison of Glasgow University.

[2] Before the age-group proportions were disturbed by emigration to America and war-losses ; but the population of Athens, especially in 431, had been affected by emigration and war-losses.

		Birth-rate (1)	Death-rate (1)	Infant death-rate (1)	Percentage of age-groups to whole population			Males and females.				Approx. percentage of males 18–59 to total.	Total Population (000's omitted).
					0–19	20–59	60–(2)	20–59		Total Population			
								M.	F.	M.	F.		
England and Wales	1871	35.5	22.3	176	45.7	46.8	7.5	22.4	23.3	48.7	51.3	24.2	22,712
	1881	34.1	19.7	141	46.3	46.4	7.3	22.2	24.2	48.7	51.3	24.0	25,974
	1891	30.8	19.7	149	45.2	47.3	7.5	22.2	25.1	48.5	51.5	24.1	29,003
	1901	28.7	17.2	146	42.4	50.2	7.4	23.9	26.3	48.4	51.6	25.8	32,528
	1911	24.5	13.8	110	40.0	52.0	8.0	24.8	27.2	48.4	51.6	26.6	36,070
	1921	20.4	12.4	78	37.1	53.5	9.4	24.9	28.6	47.7	52.3	26.6	37,887
Germany (3)	1910	28.9	16.2	—	43.5	48.7	7.8	24.0	24.7	49.3	50.7	25.8	57,798
	1925	22.1	13.3	122	36.3	54.6	9.1	25.9	28.7	48.4	51.6	27.4	62,411
Belgium	1910	22.6	15.2	—	39.7	50.9	9.4	25.3	25.6	49.6	50.4	27.1	7,424
	1920	20.4	13.4	100	34.7	55.1	10.2	27.1	28.0	49.2	50.8	28.9	7,406
Bulgaria	1910	40.2(4)	26.6(4)	—	49.5	42.2	8.3	21.5	20.7	50.9	49.1	23.4	4,338
	1920	39.0	20.8	156	47.3	44.2	8.5	21.5	22.7	50.0	50.0	23.5	4,847
	1926	32.7	17.7	147	45.9	45.9	8.2	23.3	22.6	50.1	49.9	25.5	5,479
Denmark	1911	26.0	13.4	—	42.7	47.1	10.2	22.4	24.7	48.5	51.5	24.1	2,757
	1921	22.3	11.3	82	40.6	48.8	10.6	23.4	25.4	48.7	51.3	25.2	3,268
Spain (5)	1910	32.3	23.3	—	44.6	47.6	7.8	22.8	24.8	48.6	51.4	24.6	19,996
	1920	29.8	20.2	143	41.9	48.3	9.8	23.0	25.3	48.5	51.5	24.8	21,390

	1	2	3	4	5	6	7	8	8	9	9	10	11
France	1911	17.8	19.6	—	33.9	52.5	13.6	25.4	27.1	49.1	50.9	27.0	39,192
	1921	19.3	17.2	95	31.6	54.5	13.9	25.5	29.0	47.5	52.5	27.1	38,798
	1926	18.2	16.7	89	31.0	54.6	14.4	25.7	28.9	48.0	52.0	27.3	40,228
Greece (5)	1920	23.0	16.5	86	44.9	46.3	8.8	22.4	23.9	49.7	50.3	24.2	5,017
	1928	30.1	16.5	96	43.3	47.5	9.2	23.1	24.4	49.6	50.4	25.0	6,205
Italy	1911	30.1	21.4	—	43.1	46.2	10.7	22.2	24.0	49.1	50.9	24.0	34,671
	1921	29.7	17.3	126	42.6	48.3	9.1	23.3	25.0	49.4	50.6	25.9	38,711
Holland	1909	27.9	13.7	—	44.0	47.0	9.0	23.1	23.9	49.5	50.5	24.9	5,858
	1920	25.7	10.4	64	42.4	48.8	8.8	23.9	24.9	49.7	50.3	25.9	6,865
Portugal (5)	1911	—	—	—	43.9	46.4	9.7	21.1	25.3	47.5	52.5	22.8	5,960
	1920	33.5	20.6	145	43.0	47.1	9.9	21.4	25.7	47.3	52.7	23.2	6,033

(1) The birth-rates and death-rates (cols. 1, 2, and 3) are, for pre-war years, annual rates, for post-war years, the average of 1921–5 when the census is of the year 1920, 1921 or 1925, the average of 1926–30, when the census is of a later date.

(2) Col. 7. This includes those whose age is unknown ; but their number does not disturb the percentage sufficiently to affect the figures in col. 10.

(3) Present territory (except for birth and death rates).

(4) 1909.

(5) The figures for Spain, Greece, and Portugal are in part estimates only, as enumerated in the notes to the League of Nations tables. They are sufficiently accurate for our purpose.

with intermediate rates ; (3) countries with a rapidly increasing
population (as England for most of the nineteenth century),
with a more slowly increasing population (as Germany) ; and
with an almost stationary population (as France) ; (4) countries affected by immigration (as France after the war), and
those affected by emigration (as Italy and Greece before the
war, but much less since) ; and (5) both industrial and mainly
agricultural countries.   I have included as well the post-war
figures of both belligerents and non-belligerents, to show some
of the effects of war on age-groups, though this could only be
satisfactorily illustrated by the figures for much smaller age-
groups.[1]

We have no birth-rate and death-rate figures for ancient
Athens, and not very satisfactory ones for emigration (immigration did not affect, to any appreciable extent, the numbers
of the *citizen* body in the fifth and fourth centuries) ; nor do
we know the average longevity for any period.   But we are
reasonably sure of a considerable increase in the citizen-popu-
lation between 480 and 430, in spite of much emigration, and
of some increase in the fourth century till 320.   There was
therefore an excess of births over deaths, and Athens will fall
into one of the categories of states enumerated above.   It
should also be noted that Greece is one of the few European
countries in which the sexes are approximately equal in number
(before the war there was a slight excess of males) ; and that
in all countries, there is an excess of males in the group 0—19,
and a gradually increasing excess of females in all the later
groups (quite apart from the effects of the war).

It will be seen from column 10 of the table that, in
spite of great variations in birth-rate and death-rate, before
the war only in France, Belgium and England did the males of
18—59 appreciably exceed one-quarter of the total population ;
in countries that is, not only with a comparatively low birth-
rate, but with one that has been for a generation continuously
decreasing ; also countries not much affected by emigration ;
all of which factors tend to increase the proportion of the age-
groups, 18—59.   Unless then Athens was in like case (and
who will suppose that ?) we must not assume that in 430 her
male population of 18—59 was more than 25 per cent. of the
whole ; it was very likely less, as is that of Bulgaria, Greece,
Italy (before the war), and Portugal—all much affected by

[1] For example, Germany in 1910 and 1925 (percentages of whole
population :

	0–9	10–19	20–29		30–39		40–49	
			M.	F.	M.	F.	M.	F.
1910	23.4	20.1	8.2	8.2	7.0	7.1	5.2	5.4
1925	15.8	20.5	8.9	9.5	6.4	7.8	5.9	6.5

emigration. It is therefore right to multiply by 4 ; for no modern country would 3½ be the correct factor.

But we can infer more than this. If the citizen population was increasing between 500 and 430 and between 400 and 320 (and we should remember in spite of what is often said, that the Greeks were perfectly familiar with the idea of growth of population : witness Thuc. vi 26. 2 ; Arist. *Const. Ath.* 26. 4 ; Dem. ix 40), this must have been due either to a comparatively high birth-rate or to an exceptionally low death-rate (from natural causes—excluding death from war and infanticide), or a combination of the two. Now nothing that we know of Athenian housing, medical science *and its application*, and economic conditions, would suggest that the death-rate would be low by modern standards. The wealthier classes, and men in the country, doubtless lived healthy enough lives ; but we cannot assume for all the citizens a lower death-rate (especially a lower infant death-rate) than the average of Mediterranean countries to-day. This is about 18, with about 120 infant death-rate. Assume a death-rate of 20 in ancient Athens (lower than in England before 1870), and there must have been a correspondingly high birth-rate—effective birth-rate, that is, excluding the still-born and infants killed at birth ; higher than in modern Greece ; and we reach the conclusion that there is nothing in what we know of the population of Athens in the fifth and fourth centuries to suggest that infanticide by exposure was at all common, was in any sense a regular practice.[1] And since Bolkestein, in his admirable article on the ἐγχυτριστρίαι, has disproved the only other argument for supposing that it was a regular practice (namely, the existence of a class of women employed for the purpose), we may well wonder why it was ever thought to be so. Zimmern indeed shakes his head sadly at the thought that Cimon, Pericles and Socrates are known to have had sons, but not daughters, and begs us to sympathise and understand.[2]

---

[1] The figures for Greece are actually a good deal lower than these (see above). I do not know on what evidence Myres (*Greek Lands and the Greek People*, 1910, p. 20, n. 1) says: "it is believed that hardly one in three of the children who are born in Greek lands lives to its first birthday." Later census figures from Greece do not at all support him. But if infantile mortality in ancient times was anything like this, there would be still less reason for thinking that exposure of children had any appreciable effect on the size of families. (Aristotle, *Hist. An.* vii 588 a 8, τὰ πλεῖστα δ' ἀναιρεῖται πρὸ τῆς ἑβδόμης· διὸ καὶ τὰ ὀνόματα τότε τίθενται, ὡς πιστεύοντες ἤδη μᾶλλον τῇ σωτηρίᾳ, should not be quoted as proving a high infantile death-rate. It is rightly translated by D'Arcy Thompson : "the majority of deaths in infancy occur before the child is a week old.")

[2] *Greek Commonwealth*, pp. 330 f.

He would have done better to examine his evidence ; which mostly depends on the romantic plots of tragedies and comedies (not on ordinary action in the course of the play, be it noted, but on the preliminary plot). Even if he were right, as he is not, to use this evidence as he does, yet still it would not support him. For he, like others, asserts that the exposed infants were almost always girls (or deformed children), and that the motive for exposing them was an economic one ; yet in both tragedy and comedy, exposure is not confined to girls (it is almost, as it happens, confined to boys), and the motive is never economic, but a warning oracle from on high, or because the child is illegitimate—a reason which has caused infanticide or exposure in all times and countries.[1] Besides, we might remember not only that other Athenians had daughters without boasting of their humanity, but that nearly every Athenian married ; and for that there must have been as many girls surviving from infancy as boys. Plato, when he would restrict the number of children to two per family (*Legg.* xi 930 c), yet would have one a boy, the other a girl.

This is the principal reason for rejecting any conclusions as to the size of Athenian families on the figures so carefully[2] compiled by Miss Mulder from *Prosopographia Attica*. She finds that of 347 families, no fewer than 250 had only two children. But of these 500 children, no fewer than 433 were boys; of all the children of all the families, 695 were boys, 144 were girls. Where did the Athenians find their wives ? Why was a law passed making citizens marry citizen-women only, on pain of illegitimacy of the offspring ? How could there have been an excess of women, unable to find husbands, at the end of the Peloponnesian War, a period during which, if at any time, exposure would have been common ?[3] Where, in fact, were the mothers of all these children ? We should be saved from even attempting to draw any conclusions of this kind from the evidence of the *prosopographia*, if we remembered how very little biographical detail we have even of famous

---

[1] Let us not forget the story of modern Foundling Hospitals (cf. Bolkestein, p. 239). Incidentally in the Greek drama the exposed child is always rescued, and by poor people, which does not look as though it was regarded as a burden.

[2] Carefully, yet with some errors, which seem to be all in one direction : e.g., No. 121, 5 sons (should be 4 sons and 1 daughter) ; No. 7255, 5 sons (no need to suppose the four children of Thoukritos who died young to have been all boys—Dem. lvii 28), and 4 sons and one daughter (may be 3 and 2, Nikiades II being perhaps the son of a sister of Thoukritides—*ibid* 21.).

[3] Xen. *Mem.* ii 2–6 ; and Isocr. xiv 51, the Plataean right of intermarriage with Athenians, meaning in effect marriage of Plataean men with Athenian women.

men (if it were discovered by chance that Pericles had one
or more daughters, we should be wrong to be surprised), how
much we are indebted to official records for our prosopographia:
the vast majority of names are of office-holders of one kind
or another, from a field in which women did not compete.
Even when we possess some biographical material, the *prosopographia* may mislead : we know for example of Phocion,
that he had parents, that he was twice married, and had a
son, a daughter, a brother-in-law, and a son-in-law ; yet this
family group of five men and four women is represented in
the *prosopographia* by the five men only, as we do not know
the women's names.[1]

Whether infanticide was condemned by law we do not know.[2]
But the common assertion that a father had power to repudiate
his offspring at will is disproved by the very evidence which
is used to support it. Demosthenes, *against Boeotus*, desperate
to find an argument, quotes a clause, without its context, from
a law asserting this ; but the whole conduct and the result
of this case proves the contrary ; for the oath of the mother
that the child was legitimate was final, and the father's evidence, as with us, inadmissible.[3] Infanticide, by exposure,
was certainly always known ; there are instances of it in
Hellenistic Egypt ; Polybius in a famous passage says that
the population of Greece was dying out because of the practice.[4] Even this statement we must be cautious how we use :
it may only have been true of a small and luxurious class, or
only of one part of Greece, or only of a very short period ; or
not true at all. We are very familiar with such denunciations

---

[1] Still less, though for another reason, should we rely, as Jardé
does (p. 138), on the figures of 61 families known from the orators.
They are nothing like enough on which to base statistics. Jardé is one
of those who find other persons' calculations arbitrary (as Beloch's,
that males over 18 form nearly one-third of the total population), but
can themselves make the rashest assumptions. He assumes four persons
to be the average number in an Athenian household (p. 126), and can
argue (pp. 149—150) a decline in the value of land in Greece generally
on two pieces of evidence : the values of a property in Attica c. 400
for which Lysias, xix 29, 42, gives only the vaguest information, and of
another in Thespiae in the third century (*B. C. H.* xix 1895, p. 379),
though we know nothing of the nature of either of them, except that
each included a house, not even, for example, the size of the house,
or the use to which the land was put.

[2] It is a pity that we do not know more of the γραφὴ ἀμβλώσεως
brought by Antigenes against the mother (Lysias, fr. 8). In the ordinary way we should suppose that if abortion could be condemned
(cf. the Hippocratic oath), *à fortiori* infanticide would be a crime. But
we do not know enough of the circumstances of this case.

[3] Dem. xxxix 39, xl 10–11.

[4] xxxvii 9.

F

of luxury. For Athens in the fifth and fourth centuries, we have not even that much evidence. The question has been discussed from the point of view of social ethics (which is very different from that of population) recently by Professor Cameron. His two most interesting pieces of evidence for this period are Plato, *Theaetetus*, 160 E, and Aristotle, *Politics* vii 16. 15. The first suggests the reluctant exposure of a first-born because he is a weakling, defective. The second hesitatingly advocates exposure, in order to keep population stationary, though it will be repugnant to many; it suggests to me that Aristotle is advocating a new method (for a new purpose), but is conscious that general opinion would oppose it, rather than an old one which men were beginning to dislike. Certainly we have no reason to suppose that the movement of population was sensibly affected by the practice.[1]

For the metics on the other hand multiplication of the number of men of 18—59 by 3 to 3½ should be more accurate, because they were immigrants many of whom were not long settled and often therefore without a family in Athens. A similar phenomenon is seen in modern times in countries with a large immigrant population, as America and Argentine, and in towns (in countries at least where urban development is comparatively recent[2]), in which there are relatively more men than in the rural districts, from which men of 18—40 are the first to emigrate. Compare for example the following statistics for Greece in 1920 (before the influx of refugees); of the provinces shown, Aetolia and Boeotia are pastoral and agricultural but not much affected by emigration, Arcadia, as in ancient times, and Laconia districts from which emigration is common (with a declining population), Attica dominated by the capital and its port:

---

[1] I do not know how much weight should be allowed to Isocrates' denunciation (xii 122), in its context; but it certainly does not suggest that Athenians were indifferent in the matter.

I believe the real contrast between ancient and modern times is in the provision of public orphanages and foundling hospitals. But hospitals in general were foreign to ancient Greece.

[2] Where towns are of long standing, and rich, on the other hand, as in England, there are relatively more women in them than in the country, presumably due largely to the employment of domestic servants (1096 women to 1000 men for the whole of England and Wales in 1921, 1115 in urban districts, 1165 in the County of London—Carr. Saunders and Jones, p. 4).

	Total.	Male.	Female.	Percentage of Males.
Whole country	5,536,375	2,750,904	2,785,471	49·7
Boeotia ..	74,310	36,857	37,453	49·75
Aetolia-Acarnania	190,339	93,240	97,099	49·0
Arcadia ..	125,019	58,192	66,827	46·55
Laconia-Kynuria	162,919	72,732	90,187	44·64
Attica	501,615	272,937	228,678	54·41
Athens and Peiraeus	428,824	235,768	193,056	54·98
Salonica ..	174,390	94,123	80,267	53·91
Patras	53,255	31,525	21,730	59·19

In the towns not only are men relatively more numerous, but the age-group 18—59 ; and the group 0—19 relatively less numerous than in the country.

LIST OF BOOKS AND ARTICLES REFERRED TO

BELOCH, J. *Die Bevölkerung der griechisch-römischen Welt,* 1885.

BELOCH, J. *Griechische Aufgebote :* Klio, v, 1905, pp. 341 ff.

BELOCH, J. *Griechische Geschichte,* 2nd ed., iii 2, 1923, pp. 386 ff.

BOLKESTEIN, H. *The exposure of children at Athens and the* ἐγχυτρίστριαι : *Class. Phil.* xvii, 1922, pp. 222—239.

BRENOT, A. *Recherches sur l'éphébie attique,* 1920.

CAMERON, A. *The exposure of children and Greek ethics :* *Class. Rev.* xlvi 1932, pp. 105—114.

CARR-SAUNDERS, A. M. AND JONES, D. C. *The Social Structure of England and Wales,* 1927.

CAVAIGNAC, E. *Le trésor d'Athènes,* 1908, pp. 161—176.

CAVAIGNAC, E. *Histoire de l'antiquité,* ii, 1913, pp. 1—34, 87—103.

CAVAIGNAC, E. *Population et capitale,* 1923, pp. 38—63.

CAVAIGNAC, E. *Le monde méditerranéen jusqu'au ive siècle av. J. C.,* 1929, pp. 492 ff., 702 ff.

CLERC, M. *Les métèques athéniens,* 1893.

COLIN, G. *Démosthène et l'affaire d'Harpale :* Rev. Et. Gr. xxxviii, pp. 306—49, xxxix, 31—89.

ELTER, A. *Ein athenisches Gesetz über die eleusinische Aparche.* Bonn, diss. 1914.

GERNET, L. *L'approvisionnement d'Athènes en blé :* in *Mélanges d'histoire ancienne,* 1909.

GOMME, A. W. *The Athenian hoplite force in 431. Class. Quart.* xxi, 1927, pp. 142—150.

HOMMEL, H. Art. *Metoikoi* in Pauly-Wissowa, *Realencyclopädie,* 1931.

JARDÉ, A. *Les céréales dans l'antiquité grecque,* i, 1925.

KOERTE, A. Note on the Eleusinian aparche in F. Noack, *Eleusis,* i, 1927, pp. 313 ff.

LOEPER, R. *Die Trittyen und Demen Attikas : Athen. Mitt.* xvii, 1892, pp. 319—433.

MATHIEU, G. *Notes sur Athènes à la veille de la guerre lamia-que : Rev. de Philol.* iii, 1929, pp. 159—183.

MEYER, E. *Wehrkraft, Bevölkerungszahl, u. Bodenkultur Atti-kas* in *Forschungen z. alten Geschichte,* ii. 1899, pp. 149—195.

MILCHHOEFER, A. *Untersuchung über die Demenordnung des Kleisthenes : Abhandl. Berl. Akad.,* 1892.

MILCHHOEFER, A. *Zur attischen Localverfassung : Athen. Mitt.,* xviii, 1893, pp. 277 ff.

MOEBIUS, H. *Neue Inschriften aus Attika : Ath. Mitt.* xlix, 1924, pp. 1 ff.

MULDER, J. J. B. *Quaestiones nonnullae ad Atheniensium matrimonia vitamque coniugalem pertinentes.* Utrecht, diss. 1920.

RABES, H. *Das eleusinische Zehntengesetz von* 353–2. Giessen, diss. 1924.

SARGENT, R. L. *The size of the slave population in Attica.* Urbana, 1925.

SARGENT, R. L. *The use of slaves in Greek warfare : Class. Phil.* xxii, 1927, pp. 201–12, 264–79.

SCHERLING, K. *Quibus rebus singulorum Atticae pagorum incolae operam dederint : Leipziger Studien* xviii, 1897.

SOLDERS, S. *Die ausserstädtischen Kulte und die Einigung Attikas.* Lund, 1931.

SUNDWALL, J. *Epigraphische Beiträge : Klio,* Supplbd. iv. 1906.

VAN HOOK, L. *Exposure of infants at Athens : Trans. Amer. Phil. Assoc.* li, 1920, pp. 104—145.

ZIMMERN, A. *The Greek Commonwealth,* 3rd ed., 1922.

ZIMMERN, A. *Solon and Croesus,* 1928.

INDEX OF PASSAGES IN ANCIENT AUTHORITIES, DISCUSSED OR QUOTED

Xenophon, *Hell.* i 5. 4 ff., 20 : p. 13
    ii 4. 8–9, 26 : p. 46
    iv 2. 17 : p. 7
    Mem. ii 2–6 : p. 27 n. 9,
      80 n. 2

    iii 6. 14 : p. 47 n. 1
    Vectig. 4. 14 : p. 23
      4. 24–5 : p. 20 f.
  [Xenophon], *Resp. Ath.* 1. 12, 19 :
    p. 13

INSCRIPTIONS

I.G. ii 1682 ff. : p. 44 f.

i² 76 : p. 28 n. 1
  311, 313–4 : p. 28 n. 1
  325–332 : p. 46
  373–4 : p. 39
  398 : p. 51, 55 n. 1, 56
  847 : p. 71
  897–901 : p. 49 n. 2
  900 : p. 60 n. 2
  905 : p. 46
  929, 933 : p. 49 n. 1
  970–1086 : p. 44 n. 1

ii² 1 : p. 49
  10 : p. 41 n. 3, 49
  140 : p. 28 n. 1
  204 : p. 8 n. 3
  478 : p. 9 f., 56–7, 60, 63, 69
  647 : p. 17 n. 1
  678 : p. 52 n., 57
  791 : p. 40 n. 4
  848 : p. 52 n., 59
  912 : p. 57 n. 2
  913 : p. 52 n., 55 n. 1, 56
  918 : p. 52 n., 59
  1156 : p. 9 f., 62, 67
  1193 : p. 8 n. 3
  1553–78 : p. 41 ff.
  1657–64 : p. 39
  1666, 1670–5 : p. 40
  1672 : p. 28 f.
  1697 : p. 51 n. 2
  1698 : p. 51 n. 2, 61–3, 72
  1699 : p. 51 n. 2
  1700 : p. 51 n. 2, 56–7, 59–65
  1740–3 : p. 51 n. 2
  1740 : p. 51 n. 2, 58
  1741 : p. 60
  1742 : p. 53 f., 59
  1743 : p. 62

1745–53 : p. 51 n. 2
1745 : p. 61
1746 : p. 51 n. 2, 61
1747 : p. 57
1749 : p. 57
1750 : p. 65
1751 : p. 58
1752 : p. 59
1753 : p. 52 n., 58
1835–1923 : p. 43 f.
1924 : p. 56–9, 70
1925 : p. 58–60, 70
1926 : p. 10, 53 f., 56–65, 69
  n. 2, 70
1927 : p. 70–1
1951 : p. 49 n. 2
1952 : p. 49
2366 : p. 52 n.
2370 : p. 69, 72
2372 : p. 72
2377 : p. 51 n. 2, 62 n. 2, 63
  n. 3, 72
2382 : p. 69, 72
2383 : p. 62 n. 2
2384 : p. 70, 72
2388 : p. 69, 72
2393 : p. 72
2400 : p. 64
2409 : p. 71–2
2410 : p. 69, 72
2411 : p. 60 n. 2, 72
2413 : p. 51 n. 2, 53 n. 2, 72
2423 : p. 64
2434 : p. 72
2495–2768 : p. 46

B.C.H. xix p. 379 : p. 81 n. 1

Eph. Arch. 1918 p. 73 ff : p. 9 f.,
  53 f., 59, 67 ff.

S.E.G. iii 115, 116, 122 : p. 68 n. 1